From a Deflation

From a Deflationary Point of View

PAUL HORWICH

CLARENDON PRESS · OXFORD

OXFORD
UNIVERSITY PRESS
Great Clarendon Street, Oxford OX2 6DP
Oxford University Press is a department of the University of Oxford.
It furthers the University's objective of excellence in research, scholarship,
and education by publishing worldwide in
Oxford New York

Auckland Cape Town Dar es Salaam Hong Kong Karachi
Kuala Lumpur Madrid Melbourne Mexico City Nairobi
New Delhi Shanghai Taipei Toronto

With offices in
Argentina Austria Brazil Chile Czech Republic France Greece
Guatemala Hungary Italy Japan South Korea Poland Portugal
Singapore Switzerland Thailand Turkey Ukraine Vietnam

Oxford is a registered trade mark of Oxford University Press
in the UK and in certain other countries

Published in the United States
by Oxford University Press Inc., New York

British Library Cataloguing in Publication Data
Data available

Library of Congress Cataloging in Publication Data
Data available

ISBN 0–19–925127–4 (hbk.)
ISBN 0–19–925126–6 (pbk.)

1 2 3 4 5 6 7 8 9 10

Typeset by Newgen Imaging Systems (P) Ltd., Chennai, India
Printed in Great Britain
on acid-free paper by
Biddles Ltd., King's Lynn, Norfolk

Contents

Introduction

'Deflationism' has emerged as one of the most significant developments in contemporary philosophy. It is best known as a story about truth—roughly, that the traditional search for its *underlying nature* is misconceived, since truth can have no such thing. However, the scope of deflationism extends well beyond that particular topic. For, in the first place, such a view of truth substantially affects what we should say about neighbouring concepts such as 'reality', 'meaning', and 'rationality'. And in the second place, the anti-theoretical meta-philosophy that lies behind that view—the idea that philosophical problems are characteristically based on confusion and should therefore be dissolved rather than solved—may fruitfully be applied throughout the subject, in epistemology, ethics, the philosophy of science, metaphysics, and so on.

The essays reprinted here were written in the 1980s and 1990s. They represent some of my efforts to develop and implement the deflationary outlook and they make a good case, I believe, for its power and fertility. A broad array of philosophical problems are addressed: the nature of truth, realism vs anti-realism, the creation of meaning, epistemic rationality, the conceptual role of 'ought', probabilistic models of scientific reasoning, the autonomy of art, the passage of time, and the trajectory of Wittgenstein's philosophy. But beneath this diversity there is unity at the above-mentioned meta-philosophical level: namely, in my treatment of these issues via the rooting out of confusion rather than by the construction of theories, and via the idea that supposedly 'deep' disputes are seldom to be settled in favour of one side or the other, but by the identification of shared misguided presuppositions.

In the case of our notion of *truth* this perspective fosters the view that the familiar analyses, which attempt to define it in terms of, for example, 'correspondence with facts', 'coherence amongst beliefs', or 'practical utility', all make the mistake of trying to go beyond the obvious—i.e. beyond the uncontroversial fact that each proposition (e.g. that snow is white) is equivalent to affirmations of its truth (e.g. that the proposition *that snow is white* is true). The main goal of Essay 1 ('Three Forms of Realism') is to promote the thesis—refined and defended ten years later in my book, *Truth*—that no further theory is needed, for the imagined 'hidden nature' of truth is a linguistic illusion.

An additional aim of that paper is to examine the impact of this trivialization of truth on debates between various brands of 'realism' and 'anti-realism'—debates about whether the facts within certain domains (such as ethics, arithmetic, and physics) can exist independently of our capacity to recognize them. It is suggested there, and argued more fully in Essay 2 ('Realism and Truth'), that these issues are strictly orthogonal to the line one takes on truth. Their concern, rather, is with *reductive* questions of whether the facts at issue are analysable in terms of experience and/or methodology, and with *epistemic* questions of whether knowledge of them can ever be achieved.

On the latter topic—namely, the *detection* of truth—Essay 3 ('How to Choose Amongst Empirically Indistinguishable Theories') focuses on the prospects for our being entitled to believe a given theory when there exist what would seem to be equally supported alternatives to it—alternatives whose correctness would have exactly the same import for what we are able to observe. How, for example, can our standard views about the lengths of objects be reasonable, since everything's being twice as long as it actually is would make no observable difference. Similarly, what right do we have to our normal opinions about tables, mountains, and other features of the external world, given that these opinions are derived from experience and all our experiences might be dreams? The deflationary proposal of Essay 3 is that the various competing theory-formulations in some (and perhaps all) such cases are 'potential notational variants' of one another, and that, as a consequence, the initially disquieting alternatives to our actual view of the world can be dismissed a priori.

This line of argument depends on assuming that the meaning of a word consists in our way of *using* it—and the point of Essay 4 ('Meaning, Use, and Truth') is to defend this assumption against the influential objections to it that have been advanced by Saul Kripke. The suggestion here (subsequently elaborated in my book, *Meaning*) is that Kripke's critique is undermined by its implicit dependence on a *non*-deflationary conception of truth. For his basis for concluding that our dispositions for how to use a predicate cannot constitute its meaning is that they don't 'determine', in an *explanatory* sense, the set of things of which the predicate is true. But the demand for that strong form of determination turns out to presuppose that there be some *reductive analysis* of the relation, 'w is true of x'—i.e. an inflationary account of it.

Returning to epistemology, the topic of Essay 5 ('On the Nature and Norms of Theoretical Commitment') is whether scepticism regarding a given domain of discourse (i.e. the view that justified belief within it is beyond our reach) entails that one should abandon that discourse. For might it not be useful for us to continue to make pronouncements in accordance with its rules, but without *believing* what we are saying. For example, it has been suggested by Bas van Fraassen that, although there can never be adequate grounds for believing a theory concerning unobservable entities, the standard procedures and practical purposes of science are perfectly accommodated if we take our deployment of such a theory to reflect our commitment merely to its empirical adequacy and not to its truth. (A similar proposal has been developed by Hartry Field for the case of arithmetic.) Now, as will have been argued in Essay 3, the sceptical premise that provokes this sort of 'fictionalist' recommendation may be far from compulsory. And this argument is bolstered in Essay 5, where the evidential importance of theoretical *simplicity* is brought into the picture. But the central point of this paper is to suggest that, even if the case for scepticism were in fact cogent and compelling, the proposed have-your-cake-and-eat-it response to it would be incoherent. For belief is a functionally defined state—its nature is given by its characteristic causes and effects. And so there is no possibility of acting (in thought, speech, and behaviour) just *as if* one believed certain propositions, but without really doing so. One cannot endorse scepticism, yet act in all relevant respects like a true believer.

Even from the perspective of a full-blooded non-sceptical realism, the philosophy of science still presents a variety of epistemological puzzles: e.g. Hempel's notorious raven paradox, and the question of why *diversity* of data (and not mere *quantity*) is evidentially important. A popular way of treating such problems is to invoke numerical degrees of belief and to assume that the opinions of any rational investigator must obey the laws of the probability calculus (including Bayes's Theorem). However, the correctness and relevance of that picture have often been challenged. The thesis of Essay 6 ('Wittgensteinian Bayesianism') is that, although the simple probabilistic model is indeed inaccurate in many respects, that fact about it does not detract at all from its utility in the present context. For it is not being presented as a systematic and complete *theory* of science—a contribution to naturalized epistemology. The situation rather is that many of our puzzles about evidence stem from the tendency to forget that belief is not an all-or-nothing matter; and that the Bayesian probabilistic picture—despite its various extreme idealizations—displays just the right balance of simplicity and accuracy to enable these paradoxes to be understood and disposed of.

Our sense of the passage of time has been a perennial source of controversy. Many philosophers, following Aristotle, have insisted that this sense amounts to a correct appreciation of time's basic *directional* nature. However, there appears to be no place in physics for any such model. Moreover, no one has ever been able to articulate, non-metaphorically, how exactly it could work—what it would be for time to really *flow*. The suggestion of Essay 7 ('Deflating the Direction of Time') is that the 'motion of NOW' is a linguistic/conceptual artefact, a product of how we define '*the* direction' of a process; so its existence is entirely consistent with the scientific picture of time as *intrinsically* nothing more than a symmetric one-dimensional array of instants.

A further problematic that can be fruitfully addressed from the perspective of deflationism is the conflict between 'cognitivist' and 'emotivist' accounts of normative notions such as *ought, rational,* and *good*. Are applications of these concepts similar to empirical claims in reflecting *beliefs*—beliefs that are either true or false? Or are they merely expressions of some positive or negative attitude (as urged these days by Allan Gibbard and Simon Blackburn)? In the former case, how can one explain the *motivational force* of normative commitments—i.e. our inclination to do what we think we ought to do? In the latter case, how can one make sense of *reasoning* with normative notions, which involves their appearance in logically complex constructions (e.g. 'If it's wrong to lie then it's wrong to get your little brother to lie')? Essay 8 ('Gibbard's Theory of Norms') confronts these questions and suggests that, although the defining characteristic of a normative predicate is, just as the emotivists say, the intimate (but non-reductive) relation between what someone applies it to and what they desire, that sort of conceptual role is perfectly consistent with the existence of normative reasoning, normative belief, and normative fact.

This point of view may also be adopted towards *aesthetic* judgement, as suggested in Essay 9 ('Science and Art'). The line of thought here begins with the suggestion that, unlike the sciences, the arts are not oriented towards knowledge, explanation, or understanding, but rather towards the stimulation of a characteristic form of *satisfaction* (or 'pro-feeling'). As a consequence, there are no general criteria of quality in the arts—nothing on a par with the norms of *empirical adequacy* and *simplicity*, which provide quality control in the sciences. So, as a further consequence, changes over time within the arts cannot be characterized as *progress*: Einstein improved on Newton, but Beethoven is no better than Bach. Nonetheless, aesthetic claims reflect genuine beliefs; there are genuine conflicts between people as to what is aesthetically valuable; and these opinions are genuinely true or false.

The tenth and final essay in this volume ('Wittgenstein's Meta-Philosophical Development') is explicitly focused on the perspective from which the other papers were written. It examines the fundamental role in Wittgenstein's thought of his aversion to philosophical theorizing, and argues that the crucial difference between his earlier and later work is a small but momentous modification of that attitude. His case in favour of it—his account of the new 'therapeutic' method, the work he did in that vein, and its promise of complete demystification and solid philosophical progress—are the cause of my own attachment to the deflationary point of view.

The essays appear here almost as they did when they were first published. Revision has been restricted to the elimination of typos and the occasional interpolation of clarifying material. In addition, there are some extra footnotes (marked by capital letters, 'A', 'B', etc.) to indicate subsequent work and directions in which the original ideas have struck me as in need of adjustment or elaboration.

Those ideas were hatched while I was learning the trade during my twenty-two years as a member of the Department of Linguistics and Philosophy at MIT. I owe an enormous debt of gratitude to my colleagues there—especially to Ned Block, George Boolos, Sylvain Bromberger, Dick Cartwright, Noam Chomsky, Josh Cohen, Jerry Fodor, Barbara Herman, Jerry Katz, Isaac Miller, Mickey Morgan, Bob Stalnaker, James Thomson, and Judy Thomson. I thank them for their generosity to me, and for creating a climate of unpretentiousness, rigour, and sheer pleasure in our subject.

1 Three Forms of Realism

The debate surrounding realism is hampered by an aversion to explicit formulation of the doctrine. The literature is certainly replete with resounding one-liners: 'There are objective facts', 'Truth is correspondence with reality', 'Reality is mind-independent', 'Statements are determinately either true or false', 'Truth may transcend our capacity to recognize it'. But such slogans are rarely elaborated upon. All too often the arguments, for or against, will proceed as though the nature of realism were so well-understood that no careful statement of the position is required. Consequently, several distinct and independent positions have at various times been identified with realism, and the debate is marked by confusion, equivocation and arguments at cross purposes to one another.

I think it is worth distinguishing the following three doctrines, each deserving to be regarded as a separate form of realism. For the sake of definiteness I shall write mainly about theoretical entities in science. But the points are intended to apply more generally to issues surrounding realism in other areas, concerning, for example, numbers, mental states, values, and ordinary material objects.

First, there is what might be called *epistemological realism*. This consists in the commonplace claim concerning some specified class of postulated entities that they really do exist. In this sense we are

I have benefited a great deal from conversations on these matters with Richard Boyd, William Demopoulos, Thomas Kuhn, Isaac Miller, and Hilary Putnam. Also I would especially like to thank Ned Block, George Boolos, Susan Brison, Richard Cartwright, Josh Cohen, Bernard Katz, and Esa Saarinen for reading an earlier draft of this paper and giving me good advice about how to improve it.

almost all realists about prime numbers and bacteria, but not about dragons and tachyons. No particular conception of truth is involved, nor any commitment to what the existence of the supposed entities would have to consist in. However, this brand of realism is not without philosophical interest. Concerning, for example, material things and the entities proposed by established scientific theories, the view will be opposed by the philosophical sceptic, who denies that our beliefs may be justified and is able to confine his own convictions accordingly. Thus, epistemological realists about Xs are opposed to those who, for either philosophical or non-philosophical reasons, deny that there are such things.[1]

Secondly, there is what I'll call *semantic realism*. By this I mean the anti-reductionist, anti-verificationist, anti-instrumentalist view to the effect that claims about theoretical entities should be taken at 'face value'. They are not to be understood either as mere assertions of verifiability, as covert, complex reports on observation, or as meaningless devices for the systematization of data. A semantic realist about microphysics is someone who believes that there is a body of facts[2] concerning the microscopic structure of the world, and that the object of microphysics is to discover this structure—to formulate theories and acquire evidence which will justify the belief that those theories provide a true description of that aspect of reality. He believes, in addition, that whatever microphysical facts there are need not be discoverable by us and do not depend upon our methodology.

Finally, we are left with *metaphysical realism*, a doctrine of what it *is* for such irreducible theoretical claims to be true, specifically that the concept of truth involves a primitive non-epistemic idea— for example, 'correspondence with reality'—not entirely captured

---

[1] This is not to be confounded with Putnam's Internal Realism, which is a specific empirical theory concerning the way language users map the world, and which I discuss below as the physical correspondence theory.

[2] Throughout this essay my reference to *facts* is informal; I do not mean to suggest ontological commitment to a class of such entities.

by a Tarski-style disquotation schema (*'p'* is true iff *p*). Thus metaphysical realism stands in opposition to various constructivist theories of truth (for example, intuitionism and Peirceanism) according to which the surplus meaning in 'truth' is identified with some notion of verifiability, and to the deflationist redundancy theory which denies the existence of surplus meaning and contends that Tarski's schema is quite sufficient to capture the concept. Rather, truth is held to be a substantive property of certain propositions, a property we desire our beliefs to possess and, therefore, the goal that motivates our standards of justification and our verification procedures.

My plan here is to motivate and clarify this threefold distinction and draw some conclusions from it. I'll elaborate various theses which have traditionally been used to formulate realism, including the slogans mentioned above, and examine their connection with the three distinct types of realism just sketched. I will conclude that metaphysical realism should be rejected. But this result should not trouble those whose view is merely that the facts await our investigation and exist independently of our minds and of our capacity to discover them. Such a position, which I believe is what most self-styled realists have in mind, goes no further than semantic realism. It may be sustained by means of well-known objections to verificationism and combined with a redundancy theory of truth, thereby escaping the objections to metaphysical realism.[A]

Since their work on this topic is particularly sophisticated and important, Dummett and Putnam will receive special consideration in what follows. However, although I endorse their anti-metaphysical-realist conclusion, my ideas otherwise diverge substantially from theirs. In particular they each tend to confound semantic and metaphysical

---

[A] According to the redundancy theory of truth, 'It is true that *p*' means the same as *'p'*. Since writing this essay I have come to prefer a slightly different but no less deflationary account: namely, that *'p'* and 'It is true that *p*' (and 'The proposition *that p* is true') are necessarily, and a priori, materially equivalent. See my *Truth* (2nd edn. Oxford University Press, 1998) for details.

realism and, therefore, wrongly suppose that deficiencies in the latter doctrine also count against the former. This, in turn, produces an inclination towards some form of constructivist account of truth in terms of verification; whereas I take the view that a Tarski-type schema gives us everything to which we may legitimately aspire in a theory of truth.

The assimilation of metaphysical and semantic realism derives ultimately, I suspect, from the feeling that there is something vitally important about truth that is not reflected in Tarski's theory (or in refinements of it), something that accounts for its desirability and its role in motivating our confirmation procedures. It is supposed that to understand a sentence—to attribute meaning to it—is to associate with the sentence a *condition*. This condition does or does not obtain, and thus the sentence comes to be true or false respectively. The methods devised to confirm or disconfirm the truth of the sentence are determined by what methods are suitable for finding out whether or not the condition obtains; and these methods are guided in turn by our conception of what it would be like for the condition to obtain. The question then naturally arises as to what it *is* to conceive of a condition's obtaining (or a proposition's being true). At this point the metaphysical realist contends simply that this is a primitive and unexplainable capacity that we have. Finding such a notion of truth unacceptably mysterious, and concerned lest we be left with no way of accounting for the connection between our conception of a condition's obtaining and our procedures for finding out if it does, the verificationist supposes that truth is *provability*—that our idea of what it is for a condition to obtain is just our idea of what it is for the condition to be eventually discovered. Thus, in abandoning metaphysical realism, one is led towards verificationism and away from semantic realism.

In opposing this picture and the false dichotomy it engenders between metaphysical realism and verificationism, I shall be urging an alternative point of view from which: (*a*) truth is not a graspable target in the light of which we design our confirmation practices;

(b) the obtaining of a condition is identified with the condition itself, which is in turn identified with a role in our confirmation practices—roughly, a disposition to give an associated sentence various degrees of belief depending on the circumstances; (c) the desirability of truth is explained in terms of the pragmatic value of acting on the assumption that p when and only when p. It is normally reasonable to attribute understanding—a grasp of the meanings of the sentences of a language (including unverifiable ones)—to anyone who displays the ability to use the language in accordance with community standards. Therefore, if some internal, psychological, or neurological structure turns out, upon scientific investigation, to be typically responsible for such linguistic behaviour, then possession of that structure should be identified with understanding the language. Moreover, we should describe the presence of this structure as *knowing how to use the expressions of the language, associating the right meanings with those expressions*, and in particular, *knowing what the sentences assert*, and therefore, given Tarski's schema, *knowing their truth conditions*.[3] I think that this type of use theory of meaning provides an alternative to metaphysical realism and verificationism. It combines the sound elements in each doctrine by allowing us to preserve Frege's compositional theory of sense and by accounting for the relationship between knowledge of truth-conditions and proper linguistic behaviour. At the same time, it does not involve the problematic elements—there is no mysterious notion of truth, no need for an observation/theory distinction, and no reason to retreat, as demanded by verificationism, from our ordinary attributions of understanding. This theory of meaning enables us to adopt semantic realism while avoiding any commitment to metaphysical realism.

---

[3] Although I assume that understanding a language is some kind of internal state, nothing here depends upon this assumption. Even if 'understanding' is construed behaviouristically or functionally we should still describe it as *knowing what the sentences assert*, etc.

I now turn to some traditional formulations of realism. Our threefold distinction will provide a useful framework for making sense of these slogans. Some map fairly directly on to one or another of our categories; others are ambiguous and under different interpretations will point towards different forms of realism.

The External World Formulation

First, one might have thought that realism is simply the view that there is an external reality—that there really are genes and electrons 'out there'. But it is far from clear that such beliefs distinguish realists from many of their opponents. For example, a positivist may say, 'Yes indeed, that's a gene—a real one', but then in a whisper, 'Of course, that's just to admit there are such-and-such possibilities of observation.' The point is that nearly everyone agrees there are genes and electrons, but everyone has his own different story to tell about what such a claim amounts to. Clearly, the external world formulation captures merely what I have called epistemological realism. It leaves entirely open questions about the meaning of such reality-claims and about the concept of truth involved. Thus it has no bearing upon the doctrines of semantic and metaphysical realism.

The Autonomy Formulation

A second allegedly distinguishing feature of realism is the thesis that there are facts which obtain independently of us and of our capacity to discover them. Now there is a tolerably clear sense of 'independent' according to which some facts obviously are, and some obviously are not, independent of our existence and thought. 'If there were no human beings, Disneyland would not exist, yet snow would nevertheless be white' is a view to which the proponents of almost any anti-realist position would subscribe. Just as in the case of 'There are genes and electrons', the alternative positions aim to provide distinctive accounts of such beliefs, and not to dispute them. It remains to be seen whether notions of independence can be clearly described according to which only the various forms of realist will contend that the facts are independent of our existence and thought.

If theoretical claims are reducible to observation statements or to claims about their verifiability by specified means, then there is evidently some sense in which the theoretical truths depend upon us. It is not that the truth of a theory will require the existence of observers; for a verificationist may well hold that the observable facts, and the potential verifiability of theoretical claims, would obtain even if human life had not evolved. Rather it is verificationism's account of the *nature* of the facts which exhibits the sense in which they depend upon our abilities. Thus semantic realism, in opposing the idea that truth consists in verifiability or in derivability from observation statements, automatically involves a commitment to the existence of facts whose content makes no reference to human capacities or practices, and which are in that sense autonomous.

The respect in which metaphysical realism is committed to autonomous facts is quite different and much more radical. It concerns the adequacy of the canons of justification implicit in scientific and ordinary linguistic practice—what reason is there to suppose that they guide us towards the truth? This question, given metaphysical realism, is substantial and, I think, impossible to answer; and it is this gulf between truth and our ways of attempting to recognize it which constitutes the respect in which the facts are radically autonomous. Assuming a grasp of propositions, and knowledge of *what it is* for them to have the property of metaphysical truth, it is far from clear how we could derive the ability to recognize *when* this property applies. Indeed, it is our total inability to see how this problem might be solved which should lead us to reject metaphysical realism. For if the association of propositions with sentences, plus knowledge of what it is for them to be true, do not together contribute to the explanation of linguistic behaviour (in particular, our disposition to assert certain propositions in certain circumstances), then we cannot legitimately infer those things from linguistic behaviour. But in that case we have no grounds for attributing to anyone a grasp of the metaphysical realist's notion of truth. Thus metaphysical realism involves to an unacceptable, indeed fatal, degree the autonomy of facts: there is from that perspective no reason to suppose that scientific practice provides even the slightest clue to what is true.

I suggested earlier that semantic realism should be combined with a use theory of meaning and a redundancy account of truth. This combination of views does allow us to vindicate our practice. Conformity with that practice is a component of the very behaviour from which understanding is inferred; and given the redundancy theory of truth such understanding will qualify as knowledge of truth-conditions. I am supposing here that the relationship between understanding a language and using it properly is analogous to the relationship between being water and having the complex property, *being a colourless, tasteless, liquid material that rains from the sky*. In each case the former property is normally recognized by means of the latter, although exceptions are allowed for; the former property is identified with whatever typically explains the latter manifestations; and in each case, some scientific research is required to discover the underlying nature of the former property, and to provide a theory in which its nature is described, the latter manifestations explained, and the exceptions character-ized. If this is right, then the entire content of what it is to know the truth-conditions of our sentences is captured by the idea that this knowledge contributes in a certain way towards the explanation of our practice. It follows from this that the entire practice cannot be radically misguided relative to the truth-conditions of our sentences. For if it were substantially different, the psychological or neurological structure which produces it would be different, and so we could not suppose that our sentences would be understood in the same way and associated with the same truth-conditions. Thus, contrary to metaphysical realism, truth is not radically independent of our practice.

At the same time, given the combination of views that I have suggested, truth is not *defined* in terms of our practice. Sentences that are not conclusively verifiable or falsifiable may perfectly well be understood, and their truth-conditions known, as long as our methodology provides some way of assessing and adjusting their credibility. Thus truth is independent of our practice in the respect denied by verificationism.

The Inaccessibility Formulation

What about facts which are beyond our capacity to discover? It is indeed characteristic of realism with respect to mathematics to attribute a determinate truth value even to unprovable statements. And so it may seem plausible to identify realism in general with the conviction that those statements whose assertion or denial could never be definitely justified have, nonetheless, perfectly determinate truth-values.

However, it seems wrong to insist that any form of realism depend upon the existence of such uncertainty. Even if there were no undecidable statements in mathematics one could still be a platonist. Similarly, realism in science would not be precluded by the fact, if it is a fact, that our canons of justification are sufficiently strong to invariably provide reasons to choose between rival theories. Thus a commitment to unknowable facts should not be necessary for realism. However, it certainly is sufficient. The essence of semantic realism is the denial of verificationism, and verificationism must indeed be denied before one can tolerate the existence of truth beyond our capacity to recognize it.

Metaphysical realism, on the other hand, provides quite a different perspective. If I am right about the gap between scientific methodology and metaphysical truth, then metaphysical realism is committed to an uncomfortable extent to the possibility of unverifiable truth—no truths are verifiable, or even inconclusively confirmable. However, the recognition of unverifiable truths is not peculiar to metaphysical realism and does not, therefore, entail that doctrine. There is nothing to prevent a semantic realist who endorses the redundancy theory of truth from supposing that various theoretical truths might be underdetermined by all possible evidence and, therefore, impossible to establish with certainty.

Modal Formulations

It has been suggested by Hilary Putnam that to concede that our theories might be wrong is thereby to manifest a realist understanding of truth.[4] His argument is simply that the anti-realist will identify '*p* is true' with '*p* follows from our current theory'. But in that case, the belief 'Our current theory might not be true' would entail 'Our current theory might not follow from our current theory', which no one is likely to maintain. Thus, only realists can recognize their own fallibility.

However, this reasoning underestimates the resources of anti-realism. A verificationist will certainly not sanction the identification of truth with derivability from current beliefs. He can readily assign a high credibility to various theories, and still acknowledge the distinct possibility of error.

[4] Lecture III, *Meaning and the Moral Sciences* (London: Routledge & Kegan Paul, 1978), 34–5.

In later work, Putnam has employed a variant modal formulation of realism,[5] namely, that even a methodologically ideal theory might be false—a theory which is perfectly simple, explains everything, and is, consequently, assigned maximal credibility by the canons of justification implicit in scientific practice. It is worth noting that this view is not characteristic of either semantic or epistemological realism; for there is nothing in those doctrines to encourage scepticism concerning accepted practices of confirmation. Thus a semantic realist will agree with his verificationist opponent that there is no *epistemological* possibility of the ideal theory being wrong. (Of course, everyone will accept the *logical* possibility of its falsity.) So let us assume that Putnam's intention was merely to capture the essence of metaphysical realism. In this he succeeds. Since there is no reason to expect that scientific practice approaches metaphysical truth, there is in particular no reason to think that the ideal theory is true. Thus Putnam's characterization of metaphysical realism is correct. However, as a *definition* of the doctrine, it seems deficient in two respects. In the first place, it requires reference to the dubious notion of an ideal theory. It may be that our methodological principles would never sanction the assignment of maximal credibility, and, therefore, would never recognize a theory as 'ideal', in Putnam's sense.[6] Secondly, the correctness of Putnam's characterization follows from a more general and fundamental aspect of metaphysical realism, and so it is preferable to express the doctrine by means of an account of that feature. These deficiencies are both mitigated by characterizing metaphysical realism as the view according to which truth is so inexorably separated from our practice of confirmation that we can have no reasonable expectation that our methods of justification are even remotely correct. And

---

[5] 'Realism and Reason', *Meaning and the Moral Sciences*, 125.

[6] If we don't assume that, in order to be 'ideal', a theory must be assigned maximal credibility (i.e. subjective probability equal to one), then Putnam's characterization of metaphysical realism fails. For, on any view, less than maximal credibility implies the possibility of error.

this in turn derives from an even deeper and better formulation: that truth is a non-redundant, non-epistemic indefinable quality.

The Correspondence Formulation

Some say that what is peculiar to realism is its doctrine that singular terms *refer*, sentences are sometimes *true*, and when they are, this consists in their *correspondence to the facts*. But, it is again hard to see the conflict between this tenet of realism and any of the above-mentioned brands of anti-realism. In the first place none of these theories is committed to the denial of such trivia as ' "Socrates" refers to Socrates' and ' "Snow is white" is true *iff* snow is white.' Even the instrumentalist, for whom theories are just devices for the economical organization of experience, may introduce the predicate 'is true', and put ' "Snow is white" is true' on precisely the same semantic footing as 'Snow is white.' Now our realist may attempt to salvage his individuality by emphasizing that, for him, truth is correspondence with facts. But this is useless. The others may adopt such talk of facts and agree that, by definition, what is true corresponds to a fact. Now the realist may point out that it is only on his account that truth *consists* in a correspondence with reality. But what is there to stop a semantic anti-realist from introducing 'corresponds to reality' and the schema, ' "p" corresponds to reality iff p', and then defining 'true' in terms of that notion?

The Tarskian Formulation

Let me elaborate upon the previous attempt. Suppose we try to specify the metaphysical realist notion of truth (call it 'TRUTH') by means of Tarski's definition. Thus, we say, for atomic sentences: $p_1, p_2, \ldots$

'P_k' is TRUE iff p_k

For complex sentences:

'− p' is TRUE iff 'p' is not TRUE

'$p \lor q$' is TRUE iff 'p' is TRUE or 'q' is TRUE

and so on.

This attempt fails for several connected reasons.

(A) The meaning of 'TRUE', specified in such a definition, evidently depends upon the meanings of those logical constants which are employed in the definiens. Tarski's principles remains correct even if the constants are understood intuitionistically and 'TRUE' is taken to mean 'provable'. Therefore such a characterization of TRUTH depends upon some independent way of fixing the meanings of the logical constants.

(B) We might hope to do this simply by accepting classical logic—by affirming the classical tautologies and reasoning in accordance with classical rules of inference. But we must then deal with the following two objections, from Putnam and Dummett respectively.

(1) Putnam has argued that inferential practice fails to determine the meanings of the logical constants.[7] For suppose the classical symbols are assigned intuitionistic meanings in accordance with the translation schema in the table. Now it turns out that any classical tautology, construed in this way, becomes a theorem of the intuitionistic propositional calculus. Consequently, you cannot tell from the fact that someone affirms the classical tautologies that he has assigned to the logical constants their classical meanings. According to Putnam, he may equally well be an intuitionist in disguise, who assigns to those constants the meanings prescribed in the 'Conjunction-Negation' translation. However, this is insufficient as an argument designed to show that the meanings of the constants are not fixed by inferential practice. For that practice is constituted not only by what are accepted as theorems, but also by which rules of inference are employed. Now it is true that certain

---

[7] Lecture II, *Meaning and the Moral Sciences*, 26–7.

Table 1. Conjunction–Negation Translation

classical		intuitionistic
$-p$	means	$\neg p$
$p \wedge q$	means	$p \wedge q$
$p \vee q$	means	$\neg(\neg p \wedge \neg q)$
$p \to q$	means	$\neg(\neg\neg p \wedge \neg q)$

rules would be acceptable to both the genuine classical logician and the disguised intuitionist (e.g. $p \wedge q / \therefore p$)—but not all. In particular, no disguised intuitionist may accept $--p / \therefore p$, for this transforms into the intuitionistically invalid $\neg\neg\, p / \therefore p$. Thus there are no grounds here for supposing that classical meanings are not conferred upon the logical constants simply by the acceptance of classical logic.

(2) Dummett also objects to the supposition that any consistent inferential practice assigns coherent meanings to the logical constants.[8] For in order to do this, he argues, it is necessary to assume that the rules of inference are valid, and then assign meanings (i.e. truth-conditions) to sentences by stipulating for each one that any derivation of it from true premises will qualify as a satisfaction of its truth-conditions. But then one cannot grasp the meaning of a sentence without understanding the whole language, and surveying all the ways in which it could be proved. And, according to Dummett, this form of holism is unacceptable since it renders unintelligible the functioning of language. A proper examination of this argument would go beyond the scope of this paper. I might just say that I find it unconvincing in the absence of any reason to assume that the functioning of language *is* intelligible, in Dummett's sense. Anyway, in the present context, nothing hangs on its soundness.

---

[8] *Elements of Intuitionism* (Oxford: Clarendon Press, 1977), ch.7, pp. 364–7.

(C) For, returning to the main point, even if we grant a classical construal of the logical constants which appear in Tarski's definition, that characterization nonetheless fails to distinguish the metaphysical realist and deflationist concepts of truth. Metaphysical realists disagree with deflationists in ascribing 'surplus meaning' to their notion of truth—denying that its meaning is *exhausted* by Tarski's characterization. So the remaining problem is to say what it is about TRUTH which is missed by the redundancy theory.

The Empirical Formulation

We must guard against a particular misunderstanding of our characterization of deflationism as the view that the notion of truth is completely captured by Tarski. For one may agree that truth is *defined* by Tarski, and yet disagree about whether there is anything further of interest to be discovered about the notion so specified. Thus a deflationist, in our sense, supposes that the meaning of 'true' is exhaustively specified by Tarski's characterization; but he may still acknowledge the possibility that this predicate will turn out to be co-extensive with some projectible non-semantic predicate[9]—that there will turn out to be a certain physically describable correspondence between true sentences and the states of affairs which they describe. Let us call this 'the physical correspondence theory'. What I am stressing is that this is not metaphysical realism and is not incompatible with deflationism.[B]

---

[9] This is roughly what Putnam has dubbed 'Internal Realism' and sometimes called Scientific Realism and Empirical Realism. See Lectures II and III, 'Reference and Understanding' and 'Realism and Reason' in *Meaning and the Moral Sciences*.

[B] I now think it better to reserve the term 'deflationist' for someone who accepts not only the core idea that 'true' is implicity defined by a Tarski-type schema, but also holds what is then made highly plausible: namely, that truth does not reduce to some non-semantic property.

Nevertheless, the physical correspondence theory and metaphysical realism are closely affiliated. I want to suggest that the entire plausibility of the physical correspondence theory depends upon a surplus meaning conception of truth. In the absence of such a view—realism or constructivism—there would be no reason to expect that the 'property' of truth would play a causal-explanatory role in science, and there would therefore be no reason to expect any unified physicalistic reduction of the concept.

Bear in mind the recent discussion of this issue. Tarski's definition[10] involves a distinct specification, for each atomic sentence, of the particular circumstances in which the predicate 'is true' applies to that sentence (i.e. 'Snow is white' is true iff snow is white; 'grass is green' is true iff grass is green; and so on). In other words, a basic component of this theory is a *list* of the different conditions in which different sentences are true. Hartry Field observed that definitions of this sort are unacceptable in science.[11] No one would have been satisfied with an analogous definition of valency:

(E) *(n)*(E has valency *n* iff E is potassium and *n* is + 1 or . . . or E is sulphur and *n* is −2).

Thus Field concluded that the idea of truth can be made scientifically respectable only if there can be found some unified non-semantic characteristic, indeed something physical, in which being true consists: so a complete theory of truth should contain more than just a Tarski-style definition. Then Stephen Leeds pointed out that Field's reasoning relies upon a questionable assumption.[12] Tarski's theory is inadequate only if truth is an *explanatory* property; for

[10] Cf. Tarski's 'The Concept of Truth in Formalized Languages' reprinted in his *Logic, Semantics, Metamathematics*. (Oxford University Press, 1956), 152–278. The picture of Tarski's definition presented here is highly simplified—ignoring the way that the truth of sentences depends on the reference of their parts.

[11] Cf. Field's 'Tarski's Theory of Truth', *Journal of Philosophy*, 69 (1972) 347–75.

[12] Cf. Leeds, 'Theories of Reference and Truth', *Erkenntnis*, 13 (1978), 111–29.

only then would physicalism require a *unified* physical understanding of its causal role. Finally, Hilary Putnam has claimed to have vindicated Field's criticism of Tarski by actually supplying a couple of cases in which truth does play a causal-explanatory role.[13]

Putnam's first example is that the truth of scientific theories explains their instrumental success—their capacity to predict reliably our experimental results. This is correct. However, it seems to me that the concept of truth is quite superfluous here. Clearly, any explanation whatsoever may be reformulated in such a way that the word 'true' makes an appearance. If the statement '*p*' was involved, one can simply replace it with '*p* is true'—to the same explanatory effect. But *truth* does not thereby obtain causal power. For example, what accounts for the result of the Michelson-Morley experiment is that the speed of light is absolute. Of course, one might say that the result is explained by the *truth* of Einstein's Principle; but this is not to attribute causal efficacy to the property of being true. Any explanations of the instrumental success of our theories should be located within those very theories; and though such an explanation may trivially be converted into one which employs a truth-predicate, the property of *being true* will not contribute anything of explanatory value. Thus, the instrumental success of our theories may well support instances of epistemological realism, but it does not suggest any deficiency in the redundancy theory of truth.

Putnam's second example, that upon which he puts the most weight, is his explanation of how the use of language contributes towards our success in achieving practical goals:

(1) If we have true beliefs about how to attain certain goals, we will generally attain them.

(2) We do have true beliefs about how to attain certain goals.

∴ (3) We will generally attain those goals.

---

[13] Cf. Putnam's 'Reference and Understanding', *Meaning and the Moral Sciences*, 97–119.

It seems to me that truth does indeed play an essential explanatory role in this argument. And if there were no alternative explanation then I think Putnam would have succeeded in motivating the physical correspondence theory. There is, however, an alternative which does not rely upon the concept of truth:

(1′) If we have justified beliefs about how to attain certain goals, we will generally attain them.

(2′) We do have justified beliefs about how to attain certain goals.

∴ (3′) We will generally attain those goals.

This explanation would have to be filled out with accounts of (a) how we obtain justified beliefs, and (b) how the possession of justified beliefs is conducive to the attainment of goals. To see how this could be done without recourse to the notion of truth let us focus on a simple case. Consider an elementary language containing just a single word 'Ugh', whose utterance is supposed to inform those within earshot that there is food in the vicinity. Children are taught to respond in the right way, and then said to understand the word and to justifiably believe, when they hear or say 'Ugh', that food is present. Thus the explanations of (a) and (b) would involve a psychological or neurological account of the following facts, which roughly constitute mastery of the practice: (c) that the presence of food often causes an utterance of the word 'Ugh', and (d) that hearing the word 'Ugh' brings about a search of the vicinity resulting in the acquisition of food. There is no reason to think that these causal processes are unlike other natural phenomena in requiring for their explanation the concept of truth.[C]

In challenging Putnam's examples, I am supporting Leeds's deflationist position. Moreover, I think that only a metaphysical realist or

---

[C] A better response to Putnam's argument, I now think, is to show that his explanation of success is entirely consistent with a deflationary conception of truth. The essence of the explanation is that if someone desires X and has the belief, <If I do A, then X will occur>, then he will tend to do A. And *if his belief is true* (i.e if A→X) then his desire will be satisfied. Clearly nothing beyond a deflationary schema is needed to capture the role of truth here. See *Truth* (2nd edn.), 44–6.

constructivist—a non-deflationist, who has in mind that truth is an orthodox property on a par with *red* and *round*—would be at all tempted to think that the notion may be reduced to physics. From the perspective of deflationist accounts of truth it would be a miracle if the idea turned out to have an explanatory significance for which it was not at all designed. And by the same token it would be a most remarkable coincidence if it turned out to be co-extensive with a projectible physical property. It must therefore come as no surprise to us that truth is not needed to account for the instrumental reliability of theories, the pragmatic value of language, or any other phenomenon.

Dummett's Meaning-Theory Formulation

Dummett identifies realism with the advocacy of a strong truth-conditional meaning theory.[14] A *meaning-theory* for a language is a propositional representation of what a speaker knows, and an account of how that knowledge is expressed in his practical ability to use the language. The core of a *truth-conditional* meaning-theory is a specification of conditions in which atomic sentences of the language would be true. It is either a *strong* or a *weak* truth-conditional meaning-theory, depending upon whether the notion of truth employed is metaphysical realist or constructivist.

In order to assess this characterization of realism let us consider, first, why such a meaning-theory is required, or even natural, given the metaphysical realists's conception of truth; and second, whether these views about truth and understanding should be affiliated with semantic realism.

Reformulating the first question: why should a metaphysical realist suppose that to understand a sentence is to know its TRUTH-conditions? One plausible answer to this is that, if we

---

[14] Cf. Dummett's 'What is a Theory of Meaning', part I, in S. Guttenplan (ed.), *Mind and Language*. (Oxford: Clarendon Press, 1975); and part II in G. Evans and J. McDowell (eds.), *Truth and Meaning*. (Oxford: Clarendon Press, 1976).

follow Frege in saying that the sense of a sentence is a proposition (i.e. a thought), a natural way of expressing the association of sentences and propositions is by statements of the form

'p' is true iff p.

For example, to know the meaning of 'Snow is white' would be to know that 'Snow is white' is true iff snow is white (not merely to know the truth of ' "Snow is white" is true iff snow is white', which need reflect no understanding of English). Now we may take this proposition to convey substantial information about the sentence 'Snow is white'—supposing that the meaning of 'is true iff snow is white' has been independently fixed. Alternatively we may consider it an account of what it will mean to apply the word "true" to 'Snow is white'. But if we want both information about the sentence 'Snow is white' *and* an account of the word 'true' we are in the position of someone with a single equation and two unknowns. As Dummett has often emphasized,[15] it is only because a realist rejects deflationism, and can therefore suppose that the notion of truth is grasped independently of its conformity to Tarski's schema, that he is in a position to suppose that substantial information concerning sentences is conveyed in the instances of Tarski's schema.

Thus, if we begin with the idea that the meaning of a sentence is an associated proposition, it is natural to advocate a truth-conditional meaning-theory. But this precludes the redundancy theory of truth. We must, therefore, choose between metaphysical realism and constructivism (identifying truth with verifiability). So metaphysical realism leads to the adoption of a strong truth-conditional meaning-theory. Moreover (and this is the answer to our second question), the rejection of metaphysical realism leaves us with a verificationist notion of truth and, therefore, with the rejection of semantic realism. This line of thought appears to justify both Dummett's assimilation

---

[15] Cf. Dummett's 'Truth' reprinted in his *Truth and Other Enigmas*. (Cambridge, Mass: Harvard University Press, 1978), 1–24.

of semantic and metaphysical realism, and his characterization of the compound view as the advocacy of a strong truth-conditional meaning-theory.

In response I would like to focus initially on the first step—namely the assumption that we should formulate the association of a sentence with its meaning by means of Tarski's schema. Although this strategy may be natural, it doesn't seem necessary. Why not instead describe the association by

'p' expresses the proposition that p

or by

The utterance (in certain circumstances to be spelled out) of 'p' is an assertion that p.

Neither of these methods of specifying the meaning of a sentence appears to require any notion of truth at all, and so the redundancy theory would not be precluded. Thus it becomes unclear why the idea that the meaning of a sentence is an associated proposition should force us to choose between metaphysical realism and verificationism.

Let us try a different approach. From Frege's point of view the proposition, p, is a condition whose fundamental property is either truth or falsity. Therefore, after associating the sentence 'p' with that proposition—however this connection is formulated—we may then define 'truth' for sentences by stipulating that 'p' be true if and only if the condition obtains. Thus we are giving 'p' a truth-condition. Consequently, we may describe Frege's theory as a truth-conditional meaning theory even if the meanings of sentences are not initially specified by means of Tarski's schema.

But now the question remains whether such a meaning theory would involve metaphysical realism. If, again, we follow Frege, the answer is yes.[16] Frege's view, in a nutshell, is, first, that there

---

[16] I think this view is widely held and that it is often, and not implausibly, associated with Frege. However, he may very well not have accepted it. In several places he expresses sympathy for the redundancy theory of truth.

are autonomous abstract entities, propositions, which we can apprehend; second, that each one is either true or false and that we know what it is for these properties to apply; third, that we develop the capacity to recognize the truth of certain propositions; fourth, that we associate propositions with sentences; and fifth, that we assert those sentences that have been associated with the propositions whose truth we recognize. On the basis of this picture one might well conclude that the principle

p iff it is true that p

while perfectly correct, does not capture the quality, *truth*. It provides a constraint on its attribution—if the condition, p has it, then so must the condition *it is true that p*—but it does not tell us what it is for these conditions to possess the property. Truth becomes an indefinable quality. Thus we see why metaphysical realism is associated with the advocacy of a strong truth-conditional meaning theory. It is precisely in the context of such a meaning-theory that a motive arises for the postulation of the metaphysical realist's conception of truth.

What is not so clear, however, is the answer to our second question. Why should the denial of the Fregean picture commit us to verificationism? Why can't we reject metaphysical realism and yet maintain semantic realism? I have argued above that this is both possible and desirable. In order to connect that suggestion with the present discussion, I would like to indicate, first, how a certain modification of Frege's picture avoids metaphysical realism but on pain of verificationism; and, second, how a further revision will preserve this freedom from metaphysical realism and also avoids verificationism, happily leaving us with semantic realism.

Metaphysical realism, in the context of Frege's theory as sketched above, runs into trouble at stage three. It is impossible to see how our capacity to grasp a proposition and know what it is for the proposition to be true can ever yield the ability to recognize if that proposition is true. Thus a natural modification of Frege's line of thought is to maintain that steps two and three should be inverted. Let us say, first, that we apprehend certain abstract entities—call

them *propositions;* second, that this apprehension consists in a disposition to affirm and deny them in various circumstances (in other
words, the identity of a proposition is constituted by our practice of
verifying and falsifying it); third, that we identify truth with verifiability and thereby grasp what it is to affirm or deny the *truth* of
these propositions; fourth and fifth, that we associate sentences with
the propositions and use these sentences accordingly.

I think that this verificationist revision is certainly a move in the
right direction, providing a needed connection between understanding
a language and using it properly. However, it may be improved in such a
way that the verificationism will be avoided. The modification we
should adopt is to liberalize the concept of a proposition. Instead of identifying a proposition with just one aspect of its use—namely, methods
of conclusive verification and falsification—let us associate a proposition with a broader conception of use—a role which may include methods of definite verification (but not necessarily) and also contain less
conclusive procedures of support and other inferential properties. More
specifically, the nature of this liberalization should be governed by the
constraint that precisely those sentences that we normally take ourselves to understand become associated with propositions. Any sentence
will fulfil this condition as long as our methodology provides some way
of assessing its credibility in the light of evidence.[D] Therefore, we
will associate propositions (and, given the redundancy theory, truth-
conditions) even with those sentences that are not conclusively verifiable or falsifiable. Thus we achieve semantic realism.

Finally, I would like to consider the following case against
realism, which Dummett presents in a number of places.[17]

(1) *p* is not decidable.

∴ (2) The condition for *p* to be true is not recognizable.

[D] There is perhaps no need for this qualification. Given a sentence for which no
evidence one way or the other can be found, it may nonetheless derive meaning
from the meanings of its component words—all of which appear in *other* sentences
that *are* testable.

[17] Cf. Dummett's 'The Philosophical Basis of Intuitionistic Logic', reprinted in *Truth
and Other Enigmas*, see esp. pp. 223–5. Also *Elements of Intuitionism*, 1–8 and 373–5.

∴ (3) There is no situation in which S would judge that p is true iff it is true.

∴ (4) S cannot manifest knowledge of the condition for p to be true.

∴ (5) S does not know the condition for p to be true.

∴ (6) S can attach no sense to the supposition that p is true.

∴ (7) Truth does not exist independently of our capacity to recognize it.

∴ (8) Realism is false.

∴ (9) Not even decidable statements are TRUE, in the realists' sense.

The conclusions we have reached above engender two criticisms of this argument.

First, the inference from not being able to establish when p is true to not being able to manifest knowledge of its truth-conditions is not at all compelling. All it takes to know p's truth-conditions is to understand it; and all it takes to understand p is the ability to use it in accordance with the community norms, implicit in linguistic practice, for judging, in various circumstance, the degree of confidence it should be given. We need not accept Dummett's verificationist presupposition that to understand a statement is to be capable of conclusively discerning its truth or falsity, and in that case, his argument cannot proceed beyond step (3).

Second, the argument gives the misleading impression that metaphysical realism comes to grief over undecidable statements, in particular because of its attribution of determinate truth-conditions to undecidable statements. But in fact there is absolutely no need to focus on undecidable statements. For the metaphysical realist's concepts of TRUTH and TRUTH-conditions are unacceptably obscure, even in their application to what we take to be decidable statements. There is no account of what it is to know when a sentence would be TRUE. Moreover, we have no automatic right to assume that such knowledge would be manifested in a certain form of linguistic behaviour.

We all manage to catch on to the proper (i.e. accepted) use of linguistic expressions. In particular we learn to assign credibility in ways which are sanctioned by the community at large; this practice is what generates the meanings of sentences and of the expressions which they contain. Mastering the practice is the sympton of understanding the language; and one can then be said to know what are the truth-conditions of its sentences. However, this line of thought is not open to a metaphysical realist. He wants to *reverse* the order of explanation, accounting for the behaviour in terms of the knowledge of TRUTH-conditions; and this project leaves him with two special difficulties: (1) In what does our knowledge of TRUTH-conditions consist? and (2) How does such knowledge produce linguistic skill? Now, the essential feature of the realists' TRUTH is that it is a primitive notion and, in particular, not to be explained in terms of verification. It should therefore come as no surprise that we can't answer these questions, don't understand what it is to attribute TRUTH to a sentence and have no idea what TRUTH-conditions are supposed to be.

In Dummett's argument the idea that truth is a primitive non-epistemic notion (i.e. metaphysical realism) is confounded with the idea that truth may exist beyond our capacity to recognize it (i.e. semantic realism), and then this second view is subjected to the familiar unconvincing verificationist objections. The real trouble with metaphysical realism is that the alleged notion, TRUTH, to which it subscribes cannot be made comprehensible, there being no account of that in which a grasp of it, or evidence of such a grasp, would consist.[E]

[E] I have come to think that it was a terminological error to give the label 'metaphysical realism' to the inflationary conception of truth that is criticized here. As is suggested in Essay 2, 'realism' with respect to a given domain is more naturally reserved for the position of naive common sense to the effect that there are facts in that domain that are both independent of us and yet accessible to us (i.e. semantic plus epistemological realism); and the pros and cons of that perspective have little or nothing to do with issues of truth.

2   Realism and Truth

1. *Introduction*

Is there any rational relationship between the problem of truth and the problem of realism? In particular, does the correct account of our concept of truth provide some basis for taking one side or the other in the debates between realists and anti-realists? I intend in what follows to defend a negative answer to this question—to argue that our conception of truth is epistemologically and metaphysically neutral. I will proceed by addressing three more specific questions:

First: what exactly is the problem of realism? As Michael Dummett has often emphasized, structurally similar disagreements between self-styled realists and anti-realists arise in a wide variety of domains.[1] In the philosophy of mathematics we argue about whether there are really such things as numbers; in the philosophy of science the issue concerns theoretical entities such as electrons and Chomskian I-languages; in metaphysics one wonders if there are presently any facts about what will happen in the future; and of course there is the ultimate question of realism: does the external world exist at all? My first concern will be to try to identify the common structure of the disputes that revolve around these questions.

Second: what is truth? The traditional alternatives are correspondence with reality, coherence amongst beliefs, some form of verifiability, and pragmatic utility. However, I will sketch a case for the 'deflationary' view that none of these is correct, that there is no such

---

[1] See e.g. Dummett's Introduction to *The Logical Basis of Metaphysics*, (Cambridge, Mass.: Harvard University Press, 1991).

thing as the underlying nature of truth, that our concept is adequately defined by the trivial schema, 'The proposition *that p* is true if and only if p', and that this principle accounts fully for the raison d'etre of our concept, namely, its role as a device of generalization.

Third: is there any position in the realism debate—any form of realism or anti-realism—that would not square with this deflationary story about truth. And conversely, how does deflationism affect one's stand with respect to realism? I will be arguing that the problems of realism and truth are completely independent of one another. Thus I will be opposing the generally held view, advanced by Dummett and taken over by Putnam, Kuhn, Wright, and many other writers on the topic, that there exist distinctively realist and anti-realist conceptions of truth, and that one's position in any realism debate consists in which of these notions is advocated.[2]

2. The Structure of the Realism Debates

Realism is common-sense. It holds that there *are* facts of physics, mathematics, psychology, history, and so on. It holds that such facts typically do not owe their existence to our awareness of them—or even to the possibility of our becoming aware of them. And it holds that we are, as it happens, able to acquire considerable knowledge in these domains.

Anti-realism is a philosophical critique of this cluster of naive opinions. It derives from an impression of conflict between the alleged autonomy of the facts (their independence of us) and their accessibility (the possibility of our gaining knowledge of their existence). Consequently, it seems to the anti-realist that something of our naive point of view must be given up; some philosophical move must be made. Perhaps one should concede that the facts in the domain in

[2] The independence of questions about truth from the traditional issues of realism was urged by Tarski in 'The Semantic Conception of Truth', *Philosophy and Phenomenological Research*, 4 (1943/4). It has recently been emphasized by Michael Devitt in *Realism and Truth* (Princeton: Princeton University Press, 1984 and 1991), and by the present author in *Truth* (Oxford: Blackwell, 1990).

question are mere constructions from the material of experience; perhaps one should allow, instead, that the facts lie beyond our capacity to apprehend; perhaps the right move is simply not to countenance any facts at all in the domain; or perhaps some radical account of truth, or a change of logic, will dissolve the dilemma.[A] But the essential thing, according to anti-realism, is that something must be done to resolve the tension within the realist's combination of claims, and the anti-realist proposals about meaning, knowledge, truth and logic are alternative expressions of this basic dilemma.[3]

Thus the debate between realism and anti-realism is a dispute between business-as-usual and the philosophical revision of established belief and practice. It exemplifies the meta-philosophical conflict between the Wittgensteinian idea that philosophy leaves everything as it is, and a more traditional conception of philosophy, articulated and endorsed by Dummett, that philosophy can criticize and improve existing conceptions.

I shall focus, for the sake of concreteness, on the instantiation of these issues within the philosophy of science. Here the debate concerns unobservable theoretical facts such as those postulated in cognitive science, biochemistry, and elementary particle physics. On the epistemological front the realist maintains that such theories are more or less credible, depending on the quality of our evidence; that sometimes the evidential situation is sufficiently favourable that we may be confident that our theory is true; and that we should, in such a case, believe also that the entities postulated by the theory really exist and that the statements of the theory describe facts. In addition to his common-sense epistemological opinions the realist has common-sense views about the meanings of theory-formulations. He holds that they typically concern non-observable matters—or, in

---

[A] In the terminology of Essay 1, an instrumentalist or reductionist reluctance to take the facts at face value is *semantic* anti-realism; and the view that we are not able to discover the facts is *epistemological* anti-realism.

[3] As Dummett says, 'the colourless term "anti-realism" is apt as a signal that it denotes not a specific philosophical doctrine but the rejection of a doctrine': *Logical Basis*, 4.

other words, that theoretical predicates and sentences are not translatable into observation predicates and sentences. He holds, moreover, that the theoretical facts are, in various senses, *independent* of us. Most such facts would have existed even if we had not evolved with cognitive systems good enough to conceptualize or recognize them. Indeed, it is possible, for all we know, that there actually are deep scientific facts that we are genetically incapable of discovering.

The scientific *anti*-realist is someone who thinks that this combination of common-sense views is incoherent and untenable. He cannot see how it is possible for there to be theoretical facts that, on the one hand, are within the reach of our methods of conceptualization and investigation but, on the other hand, exist independently of them. Thus, for a scientific anti-realist, the paradigm of knowledge is of *observed* facts, which are regarded as dependent upon human capacities. Such items of knowledge (and logical constructions from them) may perhaps be *reformulated* by means of linguistic conventions which introduce theoretical terms. But as soon as one attempts *genuinely* to extend this knowledge into a distinct realm of unobservable facts, then one runs into insuperable difficulties. For how could we ever recognize such facts, or even so much as comprehend them? An anti-realist is someone who believes that there is an insurmountable problem here, and is moved by this belief to renounce some element in the realist's cluster of opinions. Since this cluster may be revised in alternative ways, various distinct forms of anti-realism are possible which differ from each other with respect to where the defect in the realist position is said to lie. So we can see why, for example, Carnap, van Fraassen, Dummett, and Duhem all qualify as anti-realists, despite the fact that their positive views hardly resemble one another at all. What they share is an aversion to the realist's naive picture of facts that are both accessible and autonomous.

Early Carnap and the positivists resolve the alleged difficulty by sacrificing the autonomy.[4] They contend that theoretical expressions

---

[4] See e.g. R. Carnap, *The Logical Structure of the World* (Berkeley, Calif.: University of California Press, 1969).

are definable in terms of observation expressions—i.e. that the theoretical facts are a subset of the observational ones.

Van Fraassen, on the other hand, abandons accessibility rather than autonomy.[5] He holds, rather plausibly, that theoretical claims are not reducible to observation terms and consequently that they are not demonstrable on the basis of observable knowledge. The result, for him, is a form of scepticism. Precisely because scientific theories cannot be deduced from the data, van Fraassen denies that knowledge of theoretical facts is possible and, for that reason, denies that truth is the proper aim of science.

A third reaction to the alleged incoherence of realism is displayed by Duhem and the instrumentalists.[6] They agree that reductionism is false, but suppose that a sceptical response to this situation does not go deep enough. For the problem, they feel, is not merely the *knowledge* of theory but its very *intelligibility*, its status as potentially true or false. In denying that theory-formulations, in so far as they are not reducible to observation statements, have factual content, they reach somewhat the same conclusion as the positivists: namely that there is no distinct realm of theoretical facts.

A fourth form of anti-realism is suggested in the 'constructivist' philosophy of Dummett (although I am not sure precisely how he would apply these ideas to the philosophy of science).[7] This point of view would allow that there may be facts that go beyond what can be *reduced* to observational facts, but would deny that there can be facts that the canons of scientific verification would not enable us to discover.

Thus the debate might be characterized as follows. The scientific realist believes in various distinctions that the anti-realist denies. In particular, the realist distinguishes amongst (1) the immediately observable facts, (2) the facts that are reducible by definition to

[5] B. C. van Fraassen, *The Scientific Image* (Oxford: Clarendon Press, 1980).

[6] P. Duhem, *The Aim and Structure of Physical Theory* (Princeton: Princeton University Press, 1954).

[7] See e.g. *Elements of Intuitionism* (Oxford: Clarendon Press, 1977), *Truth and Other Enigmas* (Oxford: Clarendon Press, 1978) and *Logical Basis*.

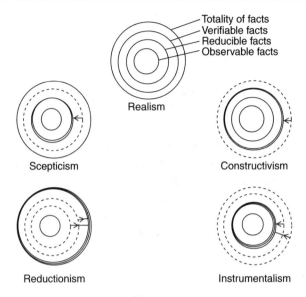

Figure 1.

observables, (3) the unobservable yet nonetheless verifiable theoretical facts, and (4) the residue consisting of undiscoverable theoretical facts. But such distinctions, according to anti-realists, involve attributing to the theoretical facts an impossible combination of autonomy and accessibility. The sceptics resolve the tension by collapsing the distinction between the verifiable and the reducible; the reductionists and instrumentalists collapse, in different ways, the distinction between the totality of facts and the reducible facts; and the constructivists deny the distinction between the totality of facts and what is verifiable. (See Figure 1.)

3. *The Problem of Truth*

The question on which I am aiming to focus concerns the relation, if any, between these positions in the realism debate and the character of truth. So let me therefore briefly address the second preliminary issue. What is truth? What definition do those of us have in mind who correctly use the truth-predicate?

The two most popular competing answers to this question have been the *correspondence theory*—roughly that 'true' means 'corresponds to a fact', which in turn is defined in terms of causal relations between words and things—and the *verification theory*—roughly that 'true' means 'provable', 'verifiable', 'ideally justifiable', 'rationally assertible', or something of the sort. However, there is no justification for insisting that the right account is given by some such traditional definition—by an account of the form 'true' means ' . . . ' For there exists a plausible alternative: namely, a version of the redundancy theory of truth (these days known as 'deflationism' or 'minimalism') according to which the rule we have in mind is simply to accept instances of the schema

The proposition *that p* is true if and only if p.

This account possesses two singular virtues. First, it explains perfectly well why we are so convinced *that the proposition that snow is white is true if and only if snow is white*, and similarly for most other propositions; and this is not such an easy matter to explain on the basis of traditional definitions of 'true'. And second, it meshes with an elegant and plausible story about why we have the concept of truth. The function of the truth-predicate, on this account (which was first articulated by Quine[8]), is not to *describe* propositions, as one might naively infer from its syntactic form, but rather to enable a certain type of generalization to be constructed. Consider, for example, the logical law,

If snow is white, then snow is white; and if quarks exist, then quarks exist; and so on . . .

We would like to be able to state this generalization in a rigorous way. And we can solve this problem with the help of the equivalence

[8] W. V. Quine, *The Philosophy of Logic* (Englewood Cliffs.Hs, NJ: Prentice Hall, 1970).

schema. For in light of those biconditionals our initial 'infinite conjunction' may be reformulated as

The proposition *that if snow is white, then snow is white* is true; and the proposition *that if quarks exist, then quarks exist* is true; and so on . . .

And this can be summarized using the ordinary universal quantifier, 'every', which generalizes over objects: i.e.

Every proposition of the form 'If p, then p' is true.

It is arguable that all legitimate and non-trivial uses of the truth-predicate are simply displays of this generalizing function.[9] If this is right, we may well suspect that traditional theories, which identify truth with one or another analysible, complex property (such as correspondence with reality, coherence, pragmatic utility, or provability), are mistaken. For the trivial equivalence schema would be necessary and sufficient for the truth-predicate to perform its function, and would provide an adequate implicit definition of 'true'. There would be no reason to expect any further account of 'what truth is'—no reason to think that truth has an 'underlying nature' remaining to be characterized.

4. Realism and Truth

This brings us finally to the central issue of this paper. Suppose you are a realist, or an anti-realist of one of the alternative types I have distinguished. Will that commitment make it necessary or natural or even slightly tempting, to embrace or reject the deflationary view of truth? And conversely, if you are persuaded by the correctness of deflationism, should you on that basis take up or avoid any particular position in the realism debate? As I said at the beginning, my answer to these questions is no. Let me now try both to justify

---

[9] I try to make such an argument in *Truth*.

this opinion and to explain why others have been inclined to see the matter differently.

Consider, to start with, the epistemological dimension of the realism debate. The realist holds, as we have seen, that inferences going from observed data to irreducibly theoretical conclusions may be perfectly rational even if there is no way of establishing that they are; the anti-realists—at least those of the van Fraassen stripe—deny this; hence they deny that theoretical knowledge is possible. Now for our purposes it is not necessary to take sides on this issue. The important thing, rather, is to see that it is not settled one way or the other by deflationism about truth. Neither the sceptical position, nor the regress and underdetermination considerations on which that position is based, make any assumptions about truth—and nor do the usual rejoinders. Thus, having been persuaded that truth is defined by the schema, 'The proposition *that p* is true if and only if p', it still remains an entirely open question whether the assertibility of theoretical hypotheses requires their reducibility to observation. And the same goes for the other dimensions of the realism/anti-realism debate: namely, whether the intelligibility of theoretical sentences requires their testability, and whether theoretical propositions are typically reducible to observation. Thus the points at issue between the realist and the various anti-realists do not concern truth, and the deflationary view of truth has no implications about what position one should take with respect to these points.

Not only is deflationism neutral with respect to the disputes between realism and anti-realism, but so are the other well-known theories of truth. One might be tempted to think, on the contrary, that the verificationist theory of truth would bear on realism by promoting the accessibility of facts at the expense of their autonomy. For one might reason that, since it is relatively easy to tell regarding, for example, the proposition that there are infinitely many stars, whether or not it is verifiable, then—given the identification of truth with verifiability—it would be equally easy to tell if that proposition is true, hence easy to tell if there are infinitely many stars. And, moreover, since the verifiability of the proposition is a fact about our methodology, then so would be the truth of the proposition, i.e. the fact that there are infinitely many stars. But both of these arguments are fallacious; for they illegitimately presume the schema, 'The proposition *that p* is true if and only if p.' And from the perspective of the verificationist analysis of truth that schema cannot be taken for granted, but stands in need of justification. Similarly, the correspondence theory of truth provides no quick path to sceptical anti-realism or to metaphysical realism. For again, those conclusions can be obtained only given the equivalence schema which, as in the previous case, will be no easier to establish than the realist or anti-realist theses it is being used to support. Thus, not only is the *right* account of truth (namely, deflationism) absolutely neutral regarding realism, but even if one adopted what I have suggested are *wrong* points of view on truth (either the correspondence or the coherence accounts) it would be a further mistake to think that any of the epistemological or metaphysical issues that constitute the realism debate would be settled.

The reason, I suspect, that truth's irrelevance to realism is not generally appreciated is that theses articulating realist and anti-realist sentiments frequently employ the notion of truth. For example:

All truths are verifiable.
Theoretical hypotheses are truth-value-less.
Science aims at truth.
No contingent statement about the future can be true.

Thus it can appear that realist and anti-realist theses are theses *about the property of truth* and that one's acceptance or rejection of them will be a reflection of what one thinks about that property.

But any such reasoning would be fallacious. It is easy to see, from the deflationary perspective, why the concept of truth is deployed in such theses; and so there isn't the slightest reason to think that an allegiance to some form of realism or anti-realism is symptomatic of a non-deflationary point of view.

In most of these cases, the notion of truth appears in the realist or anti-realist thesis in its expected role as a device of generalization. For example, a Dummettiam constructivist holds that

> If there are infinitely many stars, then it is verifiable that there are

and would want to say the same thing about all other hypotheses. His general claim can be expressed by first transforming its instances into statements such as

> If the proposition that there are infinitely many stars is true, then it is verifiable

and then employing the usual apparatus of generalization to obtain

> (x)(x is true → x is verifiable)

Or, in more familiar anti-realist lingo,

> Truth is not evidence-transcendent.

Similarly, consider the idea, which one may wish either to endorse or dispute, that science aims at truth. The idea, in particular, is that

> Scientists want it to be that they *believe* that there are infinitely many stars only if there *are* infinitely many stars

in which the notion of truth does not figure; it's only the generalization that calls for it. For in order to obtain a generalizable structure, we have to apply the equivalence schema, yielding

> Scientists want it to be that they believe that there are infinitely many stars only if it is true that there are infinitely many stars

having the form

> Scientists want it to be that they believe x only if x is true

which generalizes in the usual way to

> Scientists want it to be that they believe only what is true.[10]

---

[10] Crispin Wright has suggested (in his *Truth and Objectivity* (Cambridge, Mass.: Harvard University Press, 1992)) that the fact that we aim to believe and assert the truth constitutes an embarrassment to deflationism. But the above account of the

For a third example, consider those philosophers who hold with Aristotle that the future is open. They wish to deny all contingent propositions about the future—all propositions such as

The sea-battle will happen

and

The sea-battle will not happen.

And the basis for this position is that claims about what *will* (or *will not*) happen must be construed as claims about what *must* (or *cannot*) happen (i.e. about what is determined by current circumstances). For (so the argument sometimes goes) only given such an interpretation could such sentences be presently verifiable, and hence intelligible.

Here again, truth enters the picture only because of the desire to generalize. The equivalence schema enables us to reformulate the particular thesis as

The propsition that the sea-battle will (will not) happen is true only if it is necessary that the sea battle will (will not) happen

which generalizes in the normal way to

Future contingents are never true.[11]

Admittedly there are certain cases in which the concept of truth is deployed in formulating a realist or anti-realist thesis, where it is *not* used as a device of generalization. In these cases, however, the thesis in

---

role played by our concept of truth in articulating that norm shows, on the contrary, that it provides a paradigmatic application of the deflationary position.

[11] One often sees the Aristotelian position formulated as the thesis that future contingents are neither true *nor false*. But the claim about falsity is plausible only if one identifies the falsity of 'The sea-battle will happen' with the truth of 'The sea-battle will not happen'—which seems to me to be a mistake. Given the alleged meanings of such predictive statements, the real denial of 'The sea-battle will happen' is 'The sea battle might not happen' which is something that the Aristotelian accepts. Thus his position should be that all such predictions are *false*, not that they are truth-value-less.

question could equally well have been articulated without the notion of truth; moreover its reformulation in terms of truth is quite consistent with the deflationary position. Consider, for example, the instrumentalist idea that theoretical sentences are neither true nor false. This is the product of two claims: that theoretical sentences don't express propositions; and that propositions are the bearers of truth and falsity. Clearly, the heart of the instrumentalist position resides entirely in the first of these claims, which has nothing to do with truth. The reformulation in terms of truth is completely optional, and the assumptions about truth that it presupposes (expressed in the second implicit claim) involve nothing that goes beyond deflationism.[B]

5. Conclusion

The questions of this paper were whether there is any form of realism or anti-realism that would call for a particular theory of truth, and whether there is any conception of truth with distinctive implications in the realism debate? And the answer to both questions has turned out to be no. One's impression to the contrary stems from the fact that realist and anti-realist positions must often be formulated with the notion of truth. But the existence of such formulations tends merely to confirm the epistemologically and metaphysically neutral, deflationary theory, since they hinge merely on the generalizing function of the truth-predicate.

[B] A further form of realism with respect to a given domain may be articulated as the view that there is a notion of *truth** for that domain which involves a peculiar 'solidity', or 'robustness', or 'ontological weight'. Thus, on the face of it, the issue of whether this form of realism holds is, after all, the question of which notion of truth applies. However, there is a better way of conceiving of the issue. Suppose we can succeed in making sense of the alleged notion of 'ontological weight', and we can show that the facts in some domains, but perhaps not others, possess it. In that case, this form of realism with respect to a given domain will simply be the view that its facts possess that special character. We would then be at liberty to define a new, non-deflationary notion of *truth** as 'truth with ontological weight'. But there would be no good reason to do so—and hence no reason to conceive of 'realism' in terms of that notion.

3   How to Choose Between Empirically Indistinguishable Theories

The problem of underdetermination is a pair of related questions:

(1) Can incompatible total theories have the same testable consequences?

(2) If so, could there ever be a reason to choose between them?

1. Various Approaches to the Problem

According to positivists such as Hans Reichenbach,[1] the answer to (1) is yes, and the answer to (2) is that we may dismiss a priori all but one of the alternative candidates. Their argument relies upon the supposition that every theoretical expression is reducible, by *analytic* bridge statements, to observational terms:- if T_1 and T_2 are incompatible yet empirically equivalent, the combination of bridge statements in T_1 must be incompatible with those in T_2; but we can recognize a priori any bridge statements that conflict with analytic

I would like to thank Ned Block and David Hills for their helpful comments on an earlier draft of this paper.

[1] See 'The Nature of Geometry', in *The Rise of Scientific Philosophy* (Berkeley, Calif.: University of California Press, 1968), ch.8 and *The Philosophy of Space and Time* (New York: Dover, 1968).

truths; and so either T_1 or T_2 will be rejected a priori. I shall call this view *local conventionalism*, since it rests upon the idea that particular sentences of a theory-formulation are accepted or rejected solely as a matter of convention: in accepting S_1 (which formulates theory T_1) we reject a priori any theory, T_2, whose formulation, S_2, involves divergent bridge sentences.

Under the influence of W. V. Quine, many philosophers have renounced the conception of analytic bridge statements and therefore reject Reichenbach's solution to the problem. Hilary Putnam,[2] for example, has agreed that there may indeed be incompatible empirically equivalent theories, but has denied that the choice between them is a product of convention. Rather, he has maintained that considerations of *simplicity* must be invoked to assess the relative plausibilities of the alternative candidates. I shall call this view *inductivism* since it involves the idea that the underdetermination issue is no more than a special case of the traditional problem of induction: what makes it reasonable to choose between empirically equivalent theories are just those non-deductive (abductive) arguments which govern the choice between inequivalent, yet so-far-empirically-adequate theories.[3]

A second form of opposition to Reichenbach's positivistic approach comes from those philosophers who question the legitimacy of the observation/theory distinction. If this position, which I shall call *anti-foundationalism*, is correct, then the entire problem of underdetermination is in danger of collapse into incoherence, since the notions, such as 'observation statement', 'empirical

[2] 'The Refutation of Conventionalism', in *Mind, Language and Reality, Philosophical Papers*, (ii) (New York: Cambridge University Press, 1975). It appears that Putnam would no longer subscribe to the inductivist view that I criticize here. See 'Realism and Reason', part of *Meaning and the Moral Sciences* (London: Routledge & Kegan Paul, 1978).
[3] Another proponent of inductivism is Richard Boyd, 'Underdetermination, and a Causal Theory of Evidence', *Noûs*, 7/1 (March 1973), 1–12.

equivalence', and 'testable consequences', which appear to be indispensable in its formulation, could not be employed.

In this paper, I would like to develop an approach to the problem which diverges sharply from those three strategies which have just been described, although certain elements from each of them are preserved. I shall not take a stand on the question of analytic bridge statements, or on the legitimacy of the observation/theory distinction. Nor shall I argue that there are no cases of underdetermination for which Reichenbach's local conventionalism is correct and no cases for which Putnam's inductivism is correct. On the contrary, it seems to be that, if foundationalism is right, then there probably are *some* examples that should be handled along each of those lines. What I will attempt to establish are the following conclusions.

(*a*) There are many instances of underdetermination (including the familiar cases relating to space and time, and those employed to motivate Cartesian scepticism) for which inductivism is inadequate.

(*b*) In these cases we may know a priori (as Reichenbach thought) which, if any, of the incompatible theories is true, but we need not appeal to the positivistic doctrine of analytic bridge statements. According to what I will call *global conventionalism*, no individual bridge statement is taken to be established by convention. Nevertheless, our adoption of a whole theory-formulation will constrain the referents of its terms in such a way that the alternatives will violate the requirements of our reference-fixing practice, and can therefore be rejected a priori.

(*c*) Even if the observation/theory distinction is discarded, we may nevertheless rescue, and solve, the problem of underdetermination. For a notion of 'empirical indistinguishability' may be explicated in a way which (1) makes no reference to such a distinction, and (2) subsumes those cases to which the approach of global conventionalism is applicable.

2. Global Conventionalism

Suppose our total theory of the world, T_1, including atomic physics, is normally expressed in English by a set of sentences S_1. Thus, S_1 contains such items as:

Electrons are smaller than protons.

Now consider the sentences S_2, derived from S_1 by interchanging the expressions 'proton' and 'electron'. $\langle S_1, T_1 \rangle$ and $\langle S_2, T_1 \rangle$ are actual notational variants of each other if the terms of S_1 and S_2 are assigned referents in such a way that they both express the theory T_1. This would be achieved if we assigned to the terms 'proton' and 'electron' in S_2 those referents possessed respectively by the terms 'electron' and 'proton' in the formulation S_1 of T_1. S_1 and S_2 would then be merely alternative ways of saying the same thing. Although S_2 contains:

Protons are smaller than electrons

this apparent conflict with S_1 would be attributable to equivocation. On the other hand, we may assign to the terms of S_2 exactly those referents which they possess in the formulation S_1 of T_1. In that case S_2 will express a theory T_2 which is distinct from and incompatible with T_1. There is no equivocation, and the syntactic signs of conflict reflect a genuine difference between the theories. Moreover, assuming that none of the observation sentences of S_1 contains the terms 'electron' or 'proton', it follows that $\langle S_1, T_1 \rangle$ and $\langle S_2, T_2 \rangle$ are observationally equivalent. For if some observation sentence may be validly deduced from certain theoretical elements of S_1, it must also be deducible from the corresponding elements of S_2. Therefore, T_1 and T_2 are incompatible, empirically equivalent, total theories. How can we presume to dismiss T_2?

Reichenbach would have to say that S_1 contains certain sentences—the *definitions* of 'electron' and 'proton'—which are known a priori. So if S_2 is understood literally to express T_2, the incompatible corresponding sentences in S_2 are a priori false. Putnam, on the other hand, would appear to be faced with the hard choice between an intolerable scepticism and the implausible idea that T_1 is simpler than T_2. According to the view that I shall defend, none of these strategies is required. My thesis applied in this case is that our conventional decision to formulate our beliefs with S_1 rather than S_2 determines the a priori truth of the following statement:

> If all the characteristics that we attribute to electrons are in fact possessed by some kind of entity, then they are possessed by electrons.

But from this it follows that T_2 is false. For T_2 involves the attribution to protons (and not electrons) of all the characteristics we attribute to electrons. This approach preserves Reichenbach's idea that our rejection of T_2 is wholly a matter of convention. But it diverges in not requiring a commitment to *local* conventionalism: no particular element of our theory (e.g. electrons have negative charge) need be considered analytic or a priori. Rather it is our global conventional decision to use S_1 instead of S_2 which guarantees a priori that the theory expressed homophonically by S_2—namely, T_2—is false. Of course, this does not show that T_1 is true. All we know a priori is that, if either T_1 or T_2 is true, it must be T_1.

I am not claiming that either of the *theories* T_1 or T_2 can be made true, or false, by convention; nor that any theory is adopted by convention. Rather my position is that the choice between *formulations* S_1 and S_2 can be no more than a conventional choice about how to articulate a single theory (call it T_1). The situation is just as if S_1 differed from S_2 only in virtue of containing different definitions of some of the same words.

More specifically, an epistemological question can arise in two cases.

First, when S_1 does already in fact express our beliefs, and we are worried that S_2 might be a better view. For this case I maintain that (*a*) if S_1 were abandoned and S_2 adopted instead, then S_2 would express exactly what S_1 currently does (namely T_1); and (*b*) if S_2 is construed homophonically, it expresses an a priori false theory (call it T_2). This theory T_2 is really a priori false—not just incompatible with our theory.

Second, when neither formulation has yet been chosen. Then, whichever is selected, it will express the same theory (say T_1). And, once this selection of language has been made, the other formulation, whatever it is, will express (when construed homophonically) an a priori false theory.

A general characterization of the instances of underdetermination with which I am concerned, involves the notion of *potential notational variance*. Roughly speaking, sets of sentences S_1 and S_2 are potential notational variants when they *can* be construed so as to express the same theory. More precisely, this syntactic relation holds between S_1 and S_2 just in case there is a predicate mapping f, which transforms S_1 into S_2 and whose inverse transforms S_2 into S_1. In the example above, the predicate mapping took 'proton' into 'electron', 'electron' into 'proton', and every other expression into itself. But we are not restricted to simple interchanges. We might map '1 metre' into '2 metres', '2 metres' into '4 metres', and in general x metres into $2x$ metres, leaving every other term invariant.

Thus, if S_1 and S_2 are potential notational variant formulations, and if S_1 is understood in English to express the total theory T_1, it must be possible to construe S_2 in such a way that it also expresses T_1: S_2 *may* be interpreted so as to express T_1 in a new language whose translation into English is provided by f. The expressions of this language may be familiar English expressions, but new meanings and referents would have to be assigned to them. Alternatively, S_2 may be construed as expressing a theory in our language, English. In that case S_2 is interpreted homophonically—its terms assigned precisely those referents which they actually possess in English. Then the theory T_2 expressed by S_2 will be distinct from T_1. Moreover, if S_1 and S_2 are syntactically incompatible—if S_1

contains p and S_2 contains not-p—then T_2 and T_1 are genuinely incompatible, for the syntactic disagreement cannot be blamed upon equivocation. Now let us suppose (for the time being) that the mapping f affects only theoretical expressions. In that case the theories T_1 and T_2 constitute a case of underdetermination. Let us say that T_1 and T_2 are *isomorphic* just in case there are formulations of them which are potential notational variants of one another. I want to focus upon those cases of underdetermination which involve incompatible, empirically equivalent, *isomorphic* total theories.

In the following sections I shall first attempt to establish that in such cases all but one of the theories may be rejected a priori; second, compare this approach with those of Reichenbach and Putnam; third, suggest the applicability of global conventionalism to a range of traditional sceptical problems; and, fourth, argue for its independence of assumptions concerning the observation/theory distinction.

The main assumption of global conventionalism is that, once every one of our beliefs has been made explicit in some particular formulation, it does not remain to specify what is meant by the terms that have been employed in that formulation, since the meaning of an expression is determined by some aspect of the role it plays within the formulation of our beliefs. The role of an expression G, in the formulation $S_1(G)$ of our beliefs is specified by the set of open formulae $S_1(\phi)$ which is derived from S_1 by replacing every occurrence of G with a variable. Now to say that this role determines the referent of G is to say that, if we were to adopt some formulation $S_2(F)$—which is derived from S_1 by substituting F for G—then F would have to refer to whatever is the referent of G in our actual formulation S_1. In other words, our assumption amounts to the view that, in virtue of our decision to use $S_1(G)$ to express our beliefs, we know a priori that if something satisfies $S_1(\phi)$ then G does; it cannot happen that all our beliefs about G are in fact true of something other than G, and are not true about G. Similarly we know a priori that it is impossible for all of our beliefs about some sequence of entities $G_1, G_2 \ldots G_k$ to be untrue of those entities and yet true of some other sequence of entities.

But now the rationale for our choice among the alternative incompatible theories follows immediately. Suppose S_1 actually formulates our beliefs T_1, and that S_2 is a potential notational variant of S_1 in virtue of some predicate mapping f. Then if S_2 were adopted, the term $f(G)$ would play precisely the role that G now plays in our formulations S_1. Consequently, the referent of $f(G)$ would have to be whatever is the present referent of G. Therefore, that assignment of referents to the terms of S_2 which yields the distinct theory T_2—the homophonic assignment—must be incompatible with our reference-fixing practice. And so we know a priori that T_2 is false.

Let me repeat this argument in more formal terms. Our basic assumption is that if our actual beliefs are represented by S_1 $(G_1 \ldots G_k)$ then we have implicitly stipulated, and know a priori:

(1) $\quad \exists \langle \phi_1. \ldots \phi_k \rangle S_1(\phi_1 \ldots \phi_k \to S_1(G_1 \ldots G_k)$

Let the formulation S_2 be constructed from S_1 by some predicate mapping f which affects only the G-terms, and such that S_1 and S_2 are syntactically incompatible. And let us construe S_2 homophonically—in such a way that it expresses a theory incompatible with our own. Thus we have

(2) $\quad S_2 \to {\sim}S_1$

Moreover, given the way in which S_2 has been constructed, we know

(3) $\quad S_2 \to \exists \langle \phi_1 \ldots \phi_k \rangle S_1(\phi_1 \ldots \phi_k)$

And now it follows that S_2 is false. For given (1), we must deny either the consequent of (2) or the consequent of (3). Note particularly that (1), (2), and (3) are each known a priori. Therefore we know a priori that S_2, construed literally (i.e. T_2), is false.

S_1 and S_2 share ontological commitment to a sequence of things that satisfy $S_1(\phi_1 \ldots \phi_k)$ but disagree about whether $G_1 \ldots G_k$ is such a sequence. If we actually use S_1 we thereby implicitly adopt a reference-fixing definition (1) according to which it is. Consequently the theory expressed by S_2, interpreted homophonically, is known a priori to be false. Of course S_2 need not express a false theory. We may assign to its terms the referents they would have acquired if we had used S_2 instead of S_1. In that case S_1 and S_2 would be actual notational variants of the same theory, saying the same things in different languages.

The crucial assumption in the argument is the thesis that (1) is known a priori, which is intended to capture the idea that what we mean by our words is fixed by what we say—by how we formulate our beliefs.[4] I think that this thesis must result from any theory of reference, since our views about reference are contained in our total theory. However, I would like to provide more concrete support for the assumption by showing that it is entailed by both of the currently predominant conceptions of reference: the descriptive model associated with Frege, and Kripke's causal theory. First, if the meaning of the term G is specified by an analytic definition of the form:

$$(x)\,(Gx \equiv \ldots \ldots x \ldots \ldots)$$

then it is clearly impossible for something other than G to possess all the characteristics we attribute to G. If something satisfied $S_1(\phi)$—which, on the above assumption, would have to be equivalent to $(x)\,(\phi x \equiv \ldots x \ldots) \wedge S_1{}'(\phi)$—then that something must be G. Secondly, if the referent of the term G is taken by us to be whatever lies at the origin of a certain kind of causal chain which terminates in our usage of the word, then this is one of the very things that we believe about G. And again, nothing but G could have all the characteristics, including that one, which we attribute to G.

[4] This view is advocated by Rudolf Carnap in *Philosophical Foundations of Physics* (New York: Basic Books, 1966) and discussed by David Lewis in 'How to Define Theoretical Terms', *Journal of Philosophy*, 67/13 (9 July 1970), 427–60.

Thus, I conclude that, if the formulation S_1 is adopted, then $R(S_1) \rightarrow S_1$ becomes a priori true (where $R(S_1)$ is a Ramsey sentence derived from S_1); and if S_2 is adopted, then $R(S2) \rightarrow S_2$ becomes a priori true. Suppose someone is faced with the choice. What I have tried to argue is that this cannot be regarded as a choice between distinct theories (when S_1 and S_2 are potential notational variants). Rather, each choice will end up expressing the same theory (call it T_1). Moreover (and this can be shown either before or after some choice between S_1 and S_2 has been made), the other formulation, construed homophonically, does (if the choice *has been* made) or would (if it hasn't yet) express a theory (call it T_2) which is a priori false.

3. The Advantages of Global Over Local Conventionalism

Reichenbach's ideas on underdetermination are most clearly expressed in the context of his discussion of geometry (see n. 1). His main contention is that, in order to determine the geometry of space, one must specify, by means of coordinative definitions, what is to be meant by the geometrical terms. These will provide criteria, stated in terms of the observable behaviour of physical phenomena, for the application of geometrical predicates. Only when one is in possession of such a criterion of 'congruence'—for example, that solid objects remain the same size as they are moved in space—can one go out and measure which intervals are the same length and which lines are straight. Depending upon the criterion we adopt, we will obtain one or another formulation of geometry and physics. But unless we recognize these alternative criteria as *definitions* we may find ourselves in a serious epistemological quandary.

The trouble is that it is notoriously difficult to distinguish in a motivated way those statements about some class of entities which are true by definition from those which convey substantial information about them. Consider, for example, the theory of electrons. This contains a set of statements specifying the mass, charge, spin, and behaviour of electrons under various conditions. But it is not part of this theory that some of these claims are true by definition of 'electron', merely telling us what the theory is about. And it would be arbitrary and scientifically valueless to impose such a distinction on the theory. Similarly, no scientist feels the need to specify which statements about straight lines, if any, are merely definitions.[5]

Henri Poincaré[6] shared Reichenbach's belief that different combinations of geometry with physics might amount to no more than alternative formulations of the same total theory. But he arrived at this view not because he thought, as Reichenbach did, that the geometrical terms required operational definition, but because he felt that the axioms of alternative geometries themselves constituted alternative implicit definitions of the geometrical terms. Thus although Poincaré's view does not involve all Reichenbach's verificationist commitments (it does not require the existence of a sharp observation/theory distinction) it nonetheless manifests one of the same problematic features. That is the claim that among the sentences of a theory there is a privileged class which is true by definition. In Reichenbach's case they provide physical criteria for

---

[5] Although Quine, more than any other philosopher, is responsible for the demise of traditional empiricism, he is nonetheless one of its diehard exponents. Despite his renunciation of analytic bridge statements and the individual reducibility of theoretical claims to their observational equivalents, he retains the idea that the content of a total theory may be identified with its observational consequences. In that case, there can be no objective incompatibility between empirically equivalent total theories. In a recent paper ('Empirically Equivalent Systems of the World', *Erkenntnis*, 9/3 (Nov. 1975), 313–28) this view is refined by means of the proposal that, whenever empirically equivalent theory-formulations are potential notational variants, they should be deemed, by convention, to express the same theory. Any other translation scheme would be equally correct, he says, but the proposed method has the advantage of conformity with ordinary usage.

[6] *Science and Hypothesis* (London: Walter Scott Publishing, 1905), chs. 3–5.

congruence; for Poincaré they are the sentences of geometry. This very disagreement testifies to the element of arbitrariness involved in selecting such a class of definitions.

The virtue of global conventionalism is that it permits us to understand how we may be justified in rejecting alternative, empirically equivalent total theories, without having to assume, and justify the assumption, that some particular subset of our claims about theoretical entities are true by convention and known a priori. Both Reichenbach and Poincaré would agree that we know a priori that, if anything possesses all the characteristics we attribute to length, that thing is length. And this thesis, which is weaker than either of their views, is sufficient to guarantee that the alternative theories of geometry and physics are a priori false. For those alternatives agree about which geometrical objects exist and diverge only on the question of which of them are referred to by 'distance', 'congruence', 'straight line', etc.

A second feature of our position, which further distinguishes it from Reichenbach's, is that the rejected theories, though a priori false, need not be self-contradictory. There is no general reason to deny that these theories *could* be true, even though we know a priori that they are not. To illustrate this point, consider the theory L_2, which is identical with our actual theory of the world, L_1, except for the fact that, according to L_2, everything is twice as long as we take it to be in our theory L_1. In other words, if we actually believe of some object that it is x metres long, then L_2 says that the length of this object is $2x$ metres. Now L_1 and L_2 are observationally indistinguishable, since our measurements can merely compare lengths with one another and since L_1 and L_2 yield the same results in that regard. So how do we know that L_2 is not in fact true? The answer has, I think, been provided by Saul Kripke.[7] The standard metre bar is one metre long, by stipulation. That is how we know that it is not,

---

[7] 'Naming and Necessity', in Donald Davidson and Gilbert Harman. (eds.), *Semantics of Natural Language* (Boston: Reidel, 1971).

as L_2 says, two metres long. Nonetheless there are possible worlds in which that bar is two metres long, and some of these worlds will be described by L_2. Thus, by understanding the term 'metre' in L_2 in that sense which was determined by our stipulation, we generate a consistent theory incompatible with our theory, observationally equivalent to it, and yet known to be false. Alternatively, we could have regarded L_2 as a mere notational variant of L_1. This would have meant assigning a referent to the term 'metre' in L_2 which differs from its referent in L_1, and, if this is done properly, then L_1 and L_2 would express the same theory and be equally true.

4. The Inadequacy of Inductivism

In locating the main flaw in Reichenbach's account I follow the criticism of Hilary Putnam. However, I cannot subscribe in general to Putnam's position. He maintains that we ought to believe the simplest of the observationally adequate theories, not in virtue of any stipulation, but because it is more plausible: it involves less complicated mechanisms and is consequently more likely to be true. Putnam does not dispute that S_1 and S_2 may be understood as notational variants of the same theory. Rather his point concerns the situation where the terms of S_1 and S_2 are taken to have the same referents, thereby rendering S_1 and S_2 genuinely incompatible with each other. In that case, he says, we should regard simplicity as an indicator of truth. I do not deny that, if there are cases of empirically equivalent nonisomorphic theories, then considerations of simplicity may be invoked to assess their relative plausibility. However, when the alternatives are isomorphic—when their formulations are potential notational variants of one another—this strategy is both inapplicable and unnecessary.

It is inapplicable because in those cases there is no way to discriminate the relative simplicity of the alternative theories. In the first place, the only basis we have upon which to assess the simplicity of a theory is its formulation—the sentences used to express it—and when the alternatives are isomorphic their formulations are equally complex. Secondly, suppose that we do judge that the formulation S_1 is simpler than S_2, and conclude that T_1 is more plausible than T_2. We *could* then express T_2 with the sentences S_1 and express T_1 with S_2; and this would dictate the opposite conclusion, namely, that T_2 is more plausible than T_1. Thus, even if we do think S_1 is simpler than S_2, we cannot conclude that theory T_1 is simpler and more plausible than T_2. Thirdly, consider the justification for believing some statement P_1 of T_1 and suppose this consists of some argument—deductive or inductive or inference to the best explanation—from some set of premises, $Q_1, Q_2, \ldots, Q_n$. However good an argument this is, an equally good argument for the conclusion $f(P_1)$ may be formulated from the premises $f(Q_1)$, $f(Q_2) \ldots f(Q_n)$. If T_1 and T_2 are total theories, then Q_k is in T_1 just in case $f(Q_k)$ is in T_2. Therefore the premises of any argument for some element of T_1 will themselves be in T_1 just in case the premises for a corresponding element of T_2 will be in T_2. Thus, T_1 and T_2 have the same inductive plausibility.

Consideration of the grue problem might produce the suspicion that the simplicity of a theory depends upon more than the simplicity of its formulation, and that the quality or strength of an inductive argument depends upon something more than its syntactic form. For the grue problem arises from our intuition that the arguments

> (A) All sampled emeralds are green
> ∴ All emeralds are green

and

> (B) All sampled emeralds are grue
> ∴ All emeralds are grue

differ with respect to inductive strength although they each have the form

(C) $(x) (Kx \wedge Lx \rightarrow Mx)$
    $\therefore (x) (Kx \rightarrow Mx)$

What is wrong with this reasoning, I think, is that it involves a misrepresentation of our intuitions. It is true that discovering the premises of (A) and (B) would justify a greater degree of confidence in (A)'s conclusion than in (B)'s; however, this is because we already believe a number of things, U, about *sampling, greenness, grueness,* and *emeralds,* and so all we can say on the basis of intuition is that the arguments that differ with respect to inductive strength are

(A') $U \wedge$ All sampled emeralds are green
    $\therefore$ All emeralds are green

(B') $U \wedge$ All sampled emeralds are grue
    $\therefore$ All emeralds are grue

And we have been given no reason to think that (A') and (B') have the same logical form. On the contrary, U contains the belief:

> We have the capacity to observe whether or not an object is green without knowing what time it is and we do not have the capacity to observe whether or not an object is grue without knowing what time it is.

Therefore, the premises of (A') and (B') do not have the same logical form. Thus the grue problem provides no ground for maintaining that the simplicity and inductive plausibility of a total theory must be assessed in part on the basis of nonsyntactic considerations, and no defence against my claim that isomorphic total theories cannot be discriminated with respect to simplicity.

Fortunately, it is not necessary to invoke simplicity in order to explain how we know that T_1 is true rather than T_2: we know that T_2 is false because it conflicts with our reference-fixing practice and the conventional decision to employ S_1 rather than S_2. In summary,

Reichenbach was quite correct in maintaining that the geometry of space could be determined only relative to certain stipulations. His main mistake was to believe that these stipulations had to be localized—that the meanings of the geometrical terms had to be fixed by a particular subset of the statements of a theory—the coordinative definitions. Having rejected this extreme verificationism, it may seem natural to go one step further and conclude with Putnam that referents are not constrained at all by the formulation adopted. And this then engenders an apparently insoluble problem of underdetermination which first troubled Reichenbach and which Putnam hopes to mitigate by recourse to simplicity. However, an intermediate position, the one we have been defending, allows us to avoid the epistemological bind without Reichenbach's strong positivistic assumptions. The adoption of a whole theory-formulation both defines its subject matter and conveys substantial information.

5. Extensions of the Method

The purpose of this section is to establish and illustrate the fact that global conventionalism may be employed to resolve certain cases of underdetermination even when the alternatives are not potential notational variants of one another. Our fundamental thesis is that, if S_1 is our total theory-formulation, then we know a priori that, if a Ramsey sentence derived from S_1 is true, then S_1 is true—that is,

$$(1') \quad R(S_1) \rightarrow S_1$$

The further premises employed to justify the conclusion that S_2 (understood homophonically) may be rejected a priori were

$$(2') \quad S_2 \rightarrow {\sim}S_1$$
$$(3') \quad S_2 \rightarrow R(S_1)$$

Thus, in order to determine the class of cases in which our argument may be applied, we must identify those cases in which the premises $(2')$ and $(3')$ are satisfied.

We have considered a sufficient condition: namely, that S_2 be incompatible with S_1, and a potential notational variant of it. But this is not necessary for the satisfaction of $(3')$.

First it is enough that some *part*, K_2, of S_2 be a potential notational variant of S_1. For in that case

$$S_2 \to K_2$$
$$K_2 \to R(S_1)$$
$$\therefore S_2 \to R(S_1)$$

Second, it is sufficient that S_2 be a potential notational variant of some extension of S_1. For in that case

$$S_2 \to R(S_1 \wedge E_1)$$
$$\text{But } R(S_1 \wedge E_1) \to R(S_2)$$
$$\therefore S_2 \to R(S_1)$$

Third, $(3')$ will be satisfied when S_1 is a potential notational variant of some extension D_2 of S_2, provided this extension consists of definitions which do not supplement the ontological commitment of S_2 and which define only those terms of S_1 which are to be affected by the predicate mapping. For in that case

$$S_2 \wedge D_2 \to R(S_1)$$

But if the terms explicitly defined by D_2 appear neither in S_2 nor in $R(S_1)$, it must be that

$$S_2 \to R(S_1)$$

Moreover, it is easy to see that these three results may be combined, and so, provided $S_1 \wedge E_1$ is a potential notational variant of $K_2 \wedge D_2$ (where S_2 contains K_2), premise $(3')$ will be satisfied. Consequently, S_2 may be rejected a priori if it is incompatible with our S_1, and if some definitional extension of part of it is a potential notational variant of some extension of our S_1.

This conclusion may be applied to many familiar cases of underdetermination: the geometry of space, the metric of time, simultaneity. Let me illustrate how it resolves a well-known problem

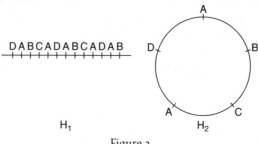

Figure 2

concerning the topology of time. Suppose H_2 includes the view that time has the structure of a closed curve whose measure is θ years. And let H_1 be the view that time has the structure of an infinite line, and the same sequence of states is repeated every θ years (see Figure 2). Thus, according to H_2, the sequence of states ABCAD occurs just once; every particular state is later than every other state. And, according to H_1, sequences of that type endlessly recur.

Now H_1 and H_2 are not potential notational variants of each other. It is possible, however, to supplement H_1 with explicit definitions in such a way that it will become a potential notational variant of an extension of H_2. Consequently, if we adopt H_2 we may reject H_1 a priori. This supplementation may be achieved as follows. First append to H_1 certain definitions D_1. For example, a *time-set* is an infinite sequence of temporal instants, each occurring θ years after its predecessor; the relation of *set-succession* between time-sets obtains when some member of one is later than some member of the other. Second, extend H_2 with claims E_2 such as: something is a temporal instant just in case it is an infinite sequence of instant-primes, each one occurring θ year-primes afterprime its predecessor-prime. Third, invoke the mapping:

f(temporal instant)   = time-set
f(later than)   = set-succeeds
f(instant-prime)   = instant
f(after-prime)   = after, etc.

to show that $H_1 \wedge D_1$ and $H_2 \wedge E_2$ are potential notational variants of each other.

6. Cartesian Scepticism

These ideas may also be applied to a broad class of traditional epistemological problems. Radical scepticism is the view that we have no reason to believe what we take ourselves to know about the external world. This position is often motivated by the description of hypothetical circumstances in which we would have precisely the experiences we do have, although our common-sense beliefs would be false. For example, we may be dreaming, our brains in a vat, stimulated from Mars, or subject to the machinations of a mischievous demon; our actual experiences would be accommodated, yet the beliefs that we derive from them would be false.

The sceptic's argument is that we have no reason to believe our theory, whose formulation S_1 includes such sentences as 'Grass is green', 'London is a large city', 'I am not in a vat', because there is an empirically indistinguishable alternative theory, formulated by S_2, and including 'A(Grass is green)', 'A(London is a large city)', 'A(I am not in a vat)'—where 'A' stands for 'It is an illusion produced by Martian stimulation (a dream) (demons) that . . . '

Now it is plausible to suspect, in light of the evident structural similarities, that our theory-formulation S_1 and the sceptic's alternative S_2 are potential notational variants. If we *do* regard S_2 as a notationally variant way of expressing our beliefs, this may be accomplished by supposing that 'A', in the language of S_2, means what we mean by 'It is true that . . .' However, the important question is whether this interpretation of S_2 is forced upon us. Is it also possible, as the sceptic must claim, to understand S_2 as the *English* expression of a theory, incompatible with ours—a theory which, for all we know, may be true?

I have suggested that, if U_2 is a notationally variant formulation of our U_1, then, if some people lived in a world in which U_2 *construed literally* was true, and yet formulated their beliefs with U_1, their beliefs would not be false, because the terms of their language would not have the meanings that they possess in English. To return to an earlier example, L_2 attributes to each object twice the length specified by our formulation L_1. L_2, constructed literally, describes a possible world. But, if someone lived in that world, yet maintained L_1, his assertions would not be false, since, by 'metre' he would pick out the quantity to which we refer using 'two metre'. Thus a world in which L_2, construed literally, is true, is a world whose inhabitants correctly describe it with L_1. Consequently, the following worry on our part would be misguided: 'Might not, for all we know, L_2 be true rather than L_1, and should we not therefore suspend our belief in L_1?'

Similarly, in a world that is correctly described in English by the sceptic's alternative theory-formulation and whose inhabitants assert our sentences S_1, the terms 'London', 'grass', 'vat', etc. do not mean what we mean by them; the beliefs expressed by their assertions are not what we mean when we produce the very same utterances; and so there is no reason to suppose that their views are mistaken. Whichever such world we occupy, our beliefs, expressed by S_1, preserve a constant truth value. For the truth-conditions of S_1 vary from world to world as a consequence of, and in systematic correlation with, the variation in the environment of its use. Therefore, the sceptic provides us with no reason to suspend our belief in S_1.

7. The Possibility of Underdetermination if Foundationalism is Incorrect

The problem of underdetermination derives from the possibility of observationally indistinguishable theories, and it can be solved, I have argued, when the theories are potential notational variants of one another. Therefore, to obtain a *general* solution it would suffice to show that empirically indistinguishable theories *must* be expressed by potential notationally variant formulations. In light of anti-foundationalist arguments—considerations which cast doubt upon the legitimacy of an observation/theory distinction—I propose that a good *explication* of what it means to say that theories are empirically indistinguishable is that their formulations are potential notational variants of one another. Let me try to defend this strategy.

A prima facie epistemological problem, concerning which of two incompatible theories is true, arises when any reason for believing one of them can be matched with a reason for believing the other. If it is assumed that the only sort of reason for believing a theory is a demonstration that the theory entails some true observation statement, then the epistemological problem emerges when two theories are shown to have the same set of observational consequences.

That assumption, however, is highly dubious. In the first place, it is notoriously difficult to give a general specification of that class of statements which we are inclined to regard as determinable by observation. This is partly because intuitions differ in regard to particular cases, such as, for example, claims made on the basis of looking through a microscope. But, more significantly, it is hard to see why we should accord such claims a privileged epistemological status. A confident observation report may be challenged and its justification seen to rest upon theoretical assumptions, even though no inference from these assumptions was causally involved in the generation of the report. Just as observations may falsify theoretical assertions, so the acquisition of theoretical knowledge may serve to undermine a class of observation claims. There is no class of statements (called 'observation statements') which are intrinsically credible—which cannot be justified in terms of further beliefs. Consequently, there is no class of statements (called 'theoretical statements') whose justification must consist in their derivation from intrinsically credible beliefs.

Thus the supposition of incompatible, observationally equivalent theories is at worst incoherent (in the absence of a clear characterization of 'observation statement') and at best fails to establish the existence of an epistemological problem, since we have no right to conclude that there could be no reason to believe one of them rather than the other.

This is not to say, however, that the sort of prima facie epistemological problem described initially cannot arise. I have not argued that there can be no pair of theories, T_1 and T_2, such that any reason for believing T_1 can be matched with a reason for believing T_2, and vice versa. I have argued against the idea that this difficulty is engendered by observationally equivalent theories. Indeed we are familiar with the conditions in which the prima facie epistemological problem *would* arise: T_1 and T_2 are competing total theories whose formulations are potential notational variants of each other. In those circumstances, as we have seen above, the premises of any argument for some element of T_1 will themselves be in T_1, just in case the premises of an equally strong argument for the corresponding element of T_2 will be in T_2. Thus any reason for believing T_1 can be matched with an equally good reason for believing T_2, and vice versa.

Thus, though the problem of underdetermination is put in jeopardy by anti-foundationalist arguments, it may be resurrected without undue violence to the intuitive idea of indistinguishability if we regard those theories as empirically indistinguishable whose formulations are potential notational variants of one another. By means of this manoeuvre the problem may not only be rescued but also solved. Given earlier results for potential notationally variant formulations, we may conclude that, though there are rival theories, empirically indistinguishable from our own, they may be rejected a priori.

4 Meaning, Use, and Truth

On Whether a Use-Theory of Meaning is Precluded by the Requirement that Whatever Constitutes the Meaning of a Predicate Be Capable of Determining the Set of Things of Which the Predicate is True and to Which it Ought to be Applied

For a large class of cases—though not for all—in which we employ the word 'meaning' it can be defined thus: the meaning of a word is its use in the language. (Wittgenstein)[1]

The purpose of this paper is to defend Wittgenstein's idea—his so-called 'use-theory' of meaning—against what is perhaps the most influential of the many arguments that have been levelled against it. I'm thinking of Kripke's critique of 'dispositionalism', which is a central component of his celebrated essay, *Wittgenstein on Rules and Private Language*.[2] Kripke argues that meaning a

For their valuable comments on earlier versions of this paper I would like to thank Ned Block, Paul Boghossian, Brian Loar, Scott Soames, Scott Sturgeon, and Timothy Williamson.

[1] *Philosophical Investigations* (Oxford: Oxford University Press, 1953), §43.

[2] Cambridge, Mass.: Harvard University Press, 1982. Kripke takes himself to sympathetically presenting Wittgenstein's view of meaning, not attacking it. Thus, despite § 43 (on which he does not comment), he does not read Wittgenstein as identifying the meaning of a word with dispositions for its use. However, the criticism of Kripke in what follows does not concern his interpretation of Wittgenstein, but solely the effectiveness of his argument against that reductive thesis.

certain thing by a word is *not* a matter of being disposed to use it in a certain way. And his argument has been well-received. Most commentators, whatever they say about Kripke's *overall* line of thought (leading up to his 'sceptical conclusion' about meaning), tend to agree at least that the use-theory has been elegantly demolished.[3] My main objective is to combat this impression.

Just what Wittgenstein himself had in mind is not entirely clear; but that's not my topic. Rather, what I want to do here is to explore and support a certain version of the use-conception of meaning— one which seems to me to have some attractive features (and which I believe can be pinned on Wittgenstein). This version involves the following interlocking elements:

(i) There are *meaning-properties*. So, for example, a certain sound has, in English, the property of meaning *dog* (or, to be more explicit, meaning *what 'dog' means in English*); a different sound has that same property in French; other English words have other meaning-properties; and so on.

(ii) Each such property has an underlying nature. The property of 'being water' is constituted by a more basic property, 'being H_2O', whose possession by something (e.g. the contents of a certain glass) explains why it has the characteristics in virtue of which we identify it as water; similarly, the property of 'meaning *dog*', for example, is constituted by an underlying property whose possession by a word explains why that word has the characteristics symptomatic of its meaning *dog*.[4]

---

[3] See e.g. Paul Boghossian, 'The Rule-Following Considerations', *Mind*, 98 (1989), 507–49; Simon Blackburn, 'The Individual Strikes Back', *Synthese*, 10 (1984), 281–301; Warren Goldfarb, 'Kripke on Wittgenstein on Rules', *Journal of Philosophy*, 82(1985), 471–88; Crispin Wright, 'Kripke's Account of the Argument Against Private Language', *Journal of Philosophy*, 81 (1984), 759–78.

[4] I am assuming that for a property U to constitute a property S it is necessary, not merely that U and S be co-extensive, but that there be a certain explanatory relationship between them: namely, that the holding of U by something explains why it has the properties that correlate with S and on the basis of which 'S's presence is

(iii) The underlying natures of meaning-properties are non-intensional. After all, the systems that display those properties are, in the end, nothing but physical objects.

(iv) The non-intensional underlying natures of meaning-properties are basic regularities of use, explanatorily fundamental generalizations about the circumstances in which words occur. For it is on the basis of assumptions about what is meant by words that we explain when they are uttered; and conversely, it is on the basis of how words are used that we infer what is meant by them. Therefore, a *basic* use-regularity could naturally explain the characteristics symptomatic of a meaning-property and would thereby satisfy the condition for constituting that property.

As I said, perhaps this isn't really Wittgenstein's view. I tend to think that it is. But my aim here is to defend the account of meaning itself and not its attribution to Wittgenstein.[5]

---

identified. Some philosophers would be inclined to say that in such cases *U* and *S* are identical, that constitution is identity. I myself find that step dubious; but nothing here hinges on whether or not one takes it.

[5] Part of the difficulty of interpreting Wittgenstein's remark is to find a reading of it that accommodates two somewhat conflicting constraints: first, that his identification of meaning with use be genuinely illuminating; and second, that it not be a controversial theory—that it conform with his therapeutic, anti-theoretical metaphilosophical outlook. One strategy of interpretation would be to note that in ordinary language the words 'meaning' and 'use' are often interchangeable: 'How is that word used?', 'The word "bank" has two uses'. But if this were what Wittgenstein had in mind, then although his thesis would indeed be uncontroversial, it would not be interesting. For ordinary characterizations of 'use' can perfectly well involve *intensional* notions—notions closely affiliated with the notion of meaning (e.g. 'It is used to refer to dogs', 'It is used to express the belief that snow is white', etc.). So we would not have achieved what Wittgenstein appears to want to achieve: namely, a demystification of meaning and related concepts. On the other hand, if one construes 'use' non-intensionally—if one insists that the use of a term be characterized in purely non-intensional (e.g. behavioural and physical) terms—then although the thesis promises to demystify meaning, it seems far from obviously correct; and to

The following discussion will be divided into three parts. To begin with I want to review briefly the distinction between two conceptions of truth: the traditional view (which I'll call *inflationary*) according to which truth is a substantive property whose underlying nature it is the job of philosophy to articulate, and a more recent *deflationary* view according to which an adequate account of truth is given (roughly speaking) by the schema

'*p*' is true iff *p*.

In the first part of my discussion I will quickly describe these competing conceptions and indicate why I think the deflationary view is correct.

In the second part I will rehearse Kripke's well known argument against the reduction of meaning-facts to facts about dispositions of use. The main thrust of this argument is that such a reduction could not accommodate the representational and normative character of meaning: the fact that we *are* disposed to apply a predicate in certain cases could not determine the set of things to which it *truly* applies and to which we *ought* to apply it.

In the third part I will show that Kripke's argument can be saved from a fallacy of equivocation (with the term 'determines') only by presupposing an inflationary conception of truth. So if, as I believe, the inflationary conception of truth is incorrect, Kripke's argument against the use-theory is unsound.

---

propound it would appear to violate Wittgenstein's meta-philosophy. Perhaps the solution to this dilemma is to suppose that Wittgenstein takes it to be obvious that conclusive criteria for what someone means lie in their behaviour, and draws the conclusion that the meaning of a word consists in non-intensional aspects of its use. He would perhaps regard the controversial character of this idea not as symptomatic of philosophical theorizing, but rather as the consequence of confusions that lead us away from what is in fact implicit in our discourse, and toward various mistaken conceptions of meaning. What follows, however, is intended merely as a defence of the use-theory of meaning, and not as an exegesis of Wittgenstein.

1. *Two Views of Truth*

It is commonly supposed that the word 'true' stands for a property that is profound, and mysterious. (Here I want to emphasize 'property', 'profound', and 'mysterious'.) That truth is a *property* almost goes without saying. We do, after all, distinguish two classes of statement: those that are true and those that aren't—so truth is what members of the first class have in common. That truth is *profound* is indicated by the striking depth, generality and variety of the principles in which it figures: truth is the aim of science, true beliefs facilitate successful action, meanings are truth-conditions, good arguments preserve truth, and so on. And, finally, that truth is *mysterious* is shown by the inability of philosophers, after hundreds of years of attempts, to say what it is. We have tried 'correspondence with reality', 'mutual coherence', 'pragmatic utility', 'verifiability in suitable conditions', and various other analyses; but every such proposal has encountered devastating objections. Either there are straightforward counterexamples, or the analysis contains notions just as problematic as truth itself. Thus truth threatens to remain a great enigma. We need to know what it is in order to assess and explain the many important principles in which it appears; but we just can't seem to make much progress.

A way out of this impasse is offered by the deflationary conception, according to which truth is not susceptible to conceptual analysis and has no underlying nature. No one doubts that the English sentence, 'snow is white', is true if and only if snow is white.[6] And, for a large range of cases, this equivalence can be generalized. Thus, instances of the so-called 'disquotational schema',

$\quad$ 'p' is true iff p,

---

[6] More accurately, one ought to speak of a sentence as *expressing a truth* rather than as *being true*; and it is in this first sense that I intend my use of the truth-predicate to be understood.

are typically uncontroversial (though exceptions must be made because of the liar-paradoxes). Traditional approaches acknowledge this but don't think of the schema as providing the sort of definition or theory that is needed and, as we have seen, attempt to achieve this end with some further principle of the form

'p' is true iff 'p' has property F

(such as correspondence to reality, provability, etc.), which is supposed to specify *what truth is*. But the deflationary view is that the search for an analysis is misguided, that our concept is exhausted by the uncontroversial schema, and that there is no reason at all to expect that truth has any sort of underlying nature.[7]

This view is best presented together with a plausible account of the *raison d' être* of our notion of truth: namely that it enables us to compose generalizations of a special sort which resist formulation by means of the usual devices—the words 'all' and 'every' and, in logical notation, the universal quantifier. Suppose, for example, we wish to state a certain form of the law of non-contradiction:

Nothing is both green and not green, or both tall and not tall, or both good and not good, and so on.

We need a single statement that will capture this 'infinite conjunction'. We can obtain it as follows. The truth schema tells us that

Nothing is both green and not green

[7] For a more detailed and exact characterization and defence of the deflationary position, as I see it, see my *Meaning* (Oxford: Oxford University Press, 1998). For other versions of the view, see W. V. Quine, *Pursuit of Truth*, (Cambridge, Mass.: Harvard University Press, 1990), ch. 5; Stephen Leeds, 'Theories of Reference and Truth', *Erkenntnis*, 13(1978), 111–29; Hartry Field, 'The Deflationary Conception of Truth', in Graham MacDonald and Crispin Wright (eds.), *Fact Science, and Morality* (Oxford: Basil Blackwell, 1986); Michael Williams, 'Do We (Epistemologists) Need a Theory of Truth?', *Philosophical Topics*, 14 (1986), 223–42.

is equivalent to

'Nothing is both green and not green' is true.

Similarly for the other conjuncts. Therefore our initial infinite list may be converted into another such list in which the same property, *truth*, is attributed to every member of an infinite class of structurally similar objects (namely sentences). Consequently, this second list can be captured as an ordinary generalization over objects:

Every sentence of the form 'Nothing is both F and not F' is true.

It is in just this role that the concept of truth figures so pervasively in logic and philosophy. Or so one might argue by showing that principles such as 'truth is the aim of science', 'true beliefs facilitate successful action', and 'good arguments preserve truth' involve the notion of truth, as in the above example, merely as a device of generalization. In so far as this can be shown, and since truth's ability to play that role requires nothing more or less than the disquotational schema, there can be no reason to suppose that truth has an underlying nature. Just because most of the properties we encounter have one, we should not assume that all do. Such an assumption about truth—the inflationary view—would seem to be a paradigmatic Wittgensteinian example of a philosophical misconception and pseudoproblem generated by an overdrawn linguistic analogy.

The distinction between inflationary and deflationary conceptions of truth is exactly paralleled by competing conceptions of *being true of* and *reference*. Thus, virtually no matter what is substituted for 'F' or 'N', it is uncontroversial that

'F' is true of something iff it is F

and

'N' refers to something iff it is identical to N

According to the deflationary point of view there is nothing more to our concepts of *being true of* and *reference* than is conveyed by our acceptance of these schemata. This is in sharp contrast to the traditional and still prevailing inflationary view according to which, given these schemata, it still remains to be said what the relations of *being true of* and *reference* really are. Some inflationary philosophers attempt to analyse these notions in terms of causal or counterfactual relations (e.g. Evans, Devitt, Stampe, Fodor); others try to do it in terms of idealized applicability (e.g. Dummett, Putnam, Wright); others attempt 'teleological' reductions (e.g. Dretske, Papineau, Millikan). But no such approach has ever seemed satisfactory. From a deflationary point of view this is only to be expected, since there are no underlying natures to be analysed here.

The deflationary conceptions of *truth, being true of,* and *reference* go hand in hand with one another. These notions are inter-definable, so any substantive analysis of one would imply substantive analyses of the others. And any argument for deflationism with respect to one of the notions (based, say, on the utility of semantic assent) will be convertible into an argument for deflationism about the other notions too.

2. *Kripke's Argument against the Use-Theory*

The core of Kripke's sceptical treatment of meaning (1982) is his argument against what he calls the dispositional theory: the view that the meaning of a word consists in dispositions regarding its use. As I reconstruct it, Kripke's reasoning is as follows:

(1) Whatever constitutes the meaning of a predicate must determine its extension (the set of things, sometimes infinite, of which the predicate is true and to which one should apply it).

(2) The use of a predicate does not determine its extension.

∴ (3) The meaning of a predicate is not constituted by its use.

There's no initial reason to question this argument's validity. And the first premise seems clearly correct, as long as we restrict our attention to terms whose extensions are context-insensitive. For, in that domain, any two synonymous predicates are co-extensional. Moreover, if predicates v and w have the same meaning-constituting property, they must have the same meaning. Consequently, if v and w have the same meaning-constituting property, then they have the same extension. In other words, just as premise (1) says, the extension of a predicate is a function of the property that constitutes its meaning.

But on what grounds does Kripke maintain the second premise: that the *use* of a predicate does *not* determine its extension? The reasoning goes roughly as follows. How *could* the use of a predicate possibly determine its extension? For if we consider the things to which we are actually disposed to apply a given word w, that set of objects is bound to diverge from the true extension of w. Our capacities are limited; mistakes occur; so w will inevitably be applied to certain things outside its extension and will fail to be applied to certain things inside its extension. In order to be able to accommodate these discrepancies it would be necessary to identify certain extremely favourable epistemological circumstances, M, such that in those ideal conditions the application of w would coincide with its extension. We would then be in a position to say that, in a sense, the use of w determines its extension; for we could identify *the use of w* with *how we are disposed to apply w in circumstances M*; and that would give us the right set. But the insurmountable difficulty with this strategy, says Kripke, is that we cannot specify the circumstances M in a satisfactory way. In order to be sure of arriving at the correct set the only characterizations of M we could offer would be

along the lines of 'circumstances in which mistakes are not made';
but that amounts to 'circumstances in which, if we mean F we apply
w to Fs', which is blatantly circular.

Paul Boghossian, who provides a sympathetic exposition of
Kripke's argument, puts the central point as follows:

> If a dispositional theory is to have any prospect of succeeding, it must
> select from among the dispositions I have for 'horse', those disposi-
> tions which are *meaning-determining*. In other words, it must charac-
> terize, in non-intensional and non-semantic terms, a property M such
> that: possession of M is necessary and sufficient for being a disposition
> to apply an expression in accord with its correctness condition.
> (Boghossian 1989: 532)

He proceeds to argue on holistic grounds (and quite persuasively)
that no such property M is specifiable.

3. *How the Use of a Predicate Determines its Extension*

A vital feature of Kripke's argument—an aspect on which, I
believe, insufficient critical scrutiny has been brought to bear in the
responses to his book—consists in the conceptions of *determination* that are deployed. According to Kripke, in order that our use of
a predicate 'determine' its extension, it must be possible to, as he
puts it, 'read off' the extension from the use. Thus he says:

> [The dispositional analysis] gives me a criterion that will tell me
> what number theoretic function φ I mean by a binary function sym-
> bol 'f' . . . The criterion is meant to enable us to 'read off' which func-
> tion I mean by a given function symbol from my disposition. (Kripke
> 1982: 26)

> According to [the dispositionalist], the function someone means is to
> be *read off* from his dispositions . . . (p. 29)

And this way of picturing the situation is repeated in Boghossian's exposition:

> it ought to be possible to read off from any alleged meaning-constituting property of a word, what is the correct use of that word. And this is a requirement, Kripke maintains, that a dispositional theory cannot pass: one cannot read off a speaker's disposition to use an expression in a certain way what is the *correct* use of that expression . . . (Boghossian (1989: 509))

But what exactly is this 'reading off' requirement? Let us look back to the way in which we saw it being applied in the justification of premise (2)—the premise that use does not determine extension. First the use-property of *w* was imagined to be something from which it follows that

> *w* would be applied (in conditions *M*) to something iff that thing is a member of *S*.

Second this relation between *w* and *S* was supposed to be what constitutes the semantic relation

> *S* is the extension of *w*.

Then, given these assumptions, it was appreciated that we would be able to *read off* the extension of any predicate from its use.

Generalizing from this example, it would seem that, in order to be able to read off the extension of any word *w* from its meaning-constituting property *U(w)*, there would have to be a fixed, uniform relation *R* satisfying the following two conditions: first, that we can deduce from *U(w)* that *w* bears *R* to some set *S*; and second, that each predicate stands in *R* to a single set, namely, to the extension of the predicate. That is to say, in order to read off the extension of *w* from its meaning-constituting property, you simply

(*a*) scrutinize the meaning-constituting property of *w*,
(*b*) infer that *w* bears *R* to set *S*,

(c) deploy the assumption that for any w and S, w bears R to S, if and only if w has extension S,[8]

(d) conclude that S is the extension of w.

It is only in this 'reading off' sense of the word 'determination' (call it 'DETERMINATION') that Kripke makes it plausible (and Boghossian even more plausible) that the use of a predicate does not DETERMINE its extension. But in that case, his argument against the constitution of meaning by use threatens to be invalidated by equivocation. For the claim of the first premise—that what constitutes meaning *does* determine extension—is uncontroversial only if we construe it (as we did above) as saying merely that any two predicates with the same meaning-constituting property are co-extensional. Thus the premises we can establish are:

(1) What constitutes meaning determines extension.

(2) Use does not DETERMINE extension.

From this, evidently, the distinctness of use from what constitutes meaning cannot be inferred.

In order to respond effectively to the present objection it would be necessary to remove the equivocation. There are two obvious strategies for attempting to do this: either argue that whatever constitutes the meaning of a predicate must DETERMINE its extension, even in the strong, 'reading off' sense; or argue that the use of a

---

[8] One might object that in order to *read off* the extension of a predicate w from the fact that w bears relation R to set S one needs merely the assumption that 'w bears R to S' is *sufficient* for 'w has extension S' and not that it is necessary; for it might be that various different relations R', R'', . . . are what determine extensions within different semantic categories of predicate. However, to the extent that we allow this flexibility and suppose the number of such extension-determining relations to be large (the limit being the supposition that each predicate bears a different relation to its extension) it becomes (a) increasingly unclear that the extension of each predicate could not be read off its meaning-constituting property (i.e. increasingly unclear that Kripke's second premise is correct); and (b) increasingly unnatural to speak of the various extensions as being 'read off'.

predicate does not determine its extension, even in the weak, functional sense. But neither of these strategies looks promising. The first one appears to be what Kripke mainly has in mind (although he also seems to sympathize with the second). However, the first strategy is affiliated with an inflationary conception of truth. For the assumption that what constitutes the meaning of each predicate DETERMINES its extension implies that there be a way of reading off a predicate's extension from whatever property constitutes its meaning. This implies, as we have just seen, that there be non-semantic necessary and sufficient conditions for *being true of*—some account of the form

w is true of the members of S iff $R(w, S)$

where $R(w, s)$ is deducible from whatever non-semantic property constitutes the meaning of w. For it is only via such an account that we can infer the predicate's extension from the property underlying its meaning. But the existence of any such theory can be taken for granted only if it is assumed that *being true of* has some non-semantic underlying nature. And that is precisely what deflationism denies.

Thus the first way of trying to remove the equivocation from Kripke's argument is motivated by an inflationary point of view. To repeat: having shown us that the *use* of a predicate does *not* DETERMINE (in the 'reading off' sense) its extension, then, in order to conclude that use does not constitute meaning, he must suppose that what constitutes the *meaning* of a predicate *does* DETERMINE its extension. He must suppose, in other words, that each meaning-constituting property relates the predicate possessing it, in a uniform way, to the extension of the predicate. But that assumption can seem plausible only if it is taken for granted that *being true of* is a substantive relation—that it has some unified naturalistic analysis and is not wholly captured by the schema

'F' is true of exactly the Fs.

So if deflationism is correct, Kripke's argument is unsound.

The only remaining hope of salvaging something from the argument would be to adopt the second strategy mentioned above. Here we drop the 'reading off' requirement, we forget strong DETERMINATION, and we reject the inflationary conception of *being true of* with which these notions are associated. Instead we operate throughout with the weak form of determination according to which the thesis that meaning determines extension is simply the thesis that synonymous predicates must be co-extensional. The second strategy is to suggest that these uncontroversial ideas about meaning are in tension with the use-theory—to show that two predicates may have the same use but different extensions.

Kripke appears to think that this can be done by means of the following thought experiment. Imagine that there is a foreign community whose use of the predicate 'quus' has been, always will be, and would, in all hypothetical circumstances, be just the same as our use of 'plus', but whose predicate is true of a slightly different set of triples of numbers—the difference concerning only numbers that are so ungraspably huge that neither we nor they have the capacity to talk about them. If this really is possible, then usage doesn't determine extension (even in the weak, non 'reading off' sense) and so cannot constitute meaning.

The trouble with this argument is that it assumes the very thing that it is supposed to establish; namely, that a word whose use is *exactly* the same as the use of our word 'plus' might nonetheless have a different extension. To insist, without justification, on there being such a possibility is simply to beg the question against the use-theory of meaning. What does seem intuitively right is that there are possible *complex* expressions—definable in terms of 'plus'—whose extensions diverge from that of 'plus' in the slight way imagined. But no complex expression—since it will inevitably bear certain use-relations to its constituents—can have exactly the same use as a primitive expression. Therefore, in order to construct his counterexample to the use-theory, Kripke must assume that the term 'quus' satisfies the following three conditions: (1) that it be a *primitive* term (on a par with 'plus'); (2) that it be co-extensive with one of those possible, complex expressions whose extension diverges very slightly and remotely from that of 'plus'; and (3) that its use (including the absence of dispositions regarding the divergent cases) be identical to our use of 'plus'. But it is plausible to suppose that 'quus' would acquire such an extension only if either it were defined in terms of some word meaning the same as 'plus' or it were applied in some *definite* way to certain triples that, given our limitations, are beyond our definite range of application of 'plus'; and in neither of these cases would it be correct to say that the use of 'quus' is *exactly* like our use of 'plus'. Thus what Kripke needs to assume in order to construct a counterexample is intuitively implausible and simply begs the question against the use-theory of meaning.[9]

But why, one may be tempted to insist, should our dispositions for the use of 'plus' be associated with *plus* rather than one of the other functions with which these dispositions are consistent? It appears to be impossible to explain, on the basis of our practice with a word, why it should mean what it does, and why it should happen to apply to one set of entities rather than another.[10]

---

[9] It might be thought that my claim that Kripke is begging the question is itself begging the question: i.e. that it reflects an unjustified assumption on my part about who has the burden of proof. But such a complaint would neglect the facts (*a*) that there are independent reasons (sketched at the beginning of this paper) for taking the use-theory very seriously; and (*b*) that Kripke does not so much as hint at what factors, other than use, might underpin the difference between meaning *plus* and *quus*—let alone justify any such assumption. Could Kripke be making the very mistake he so insightfully exposes in *Naming and Necessity*? For, just as it is 'conceivable' that H_2O constitute something other than water (exhibiting different observable characteristics), so it may be conceivable that our basic use of 'plus' go with a different meaning. But in neither case do we have *metaphysical* possibility.

[10] Here we must of course separate the epistemological issue—given the use of a predicate, what puts us in a position to say that its extension is such-and-such rather than so-and-so?—and the explanatory issue—why, given the use of predicate, is its extension such-and-such rather than so-and-so? The question that is raised and addressed in the text concerns explanation, but let me say a quick word here about the epistemological situation.

Well, yes and no. For suppose that the property

  w means *plus*

is constituted by the property

  w's use is so-and-so.

In that case we surely do explain why a certain word means *plus* if we point out that its use is so-and-so. This is not to say, however, that we can explain *why* this particular use-property constitutes that particular meaning-property. And in fact I think that nothing of the sort can reasonably be expected. For such an explanation could be given only if there were some general principle by which a term's meaning could be extracted from a characterization of its use. Thus the prospect of such an explanation goes hand in hand with the reading off requirement, with strong DETERMINATION of extensions by meanings, and with the inflationary conception of truth.

Notice moreover that the existence of an inexplicable constitutive relation between properties is perfectly normal. One can't explain why it is that water is made of H_2O, or why it is that the underlying nature of redness is to reflect certain wavelengths of light. The best we can do, in such cases, is to *justify* the thesis of

---

In the case of a predicate of our own language (e.g. 'horse'), we master its use (without necessarily being able to characterize that use explicitly) and we arrive at our knowledge of its extension by means of the stipulation

'horse' is true of exactly the horses

which partially defines 'is true of'. We do not infer the extension of 'horse' from its use. The situation is rather that we apply the extension-determining stipulation only to those predicates that we use. Thus it is by definition that we know that 'horse' is true of horses, and not of 'quorses'.

In the case of foreign words the situation is slightly different. Their extensions are determined by principles such as

w means the same as 'horse' → (w is true of exactly the horses).

Therefore the knowledge that a foreign word has the same use and therefore the same meaning as 'horse' will be the basis for inferring its extension.

constitution by showing how the underlying property gives rise to the characteristic symptoms of the more superficial one. In the same way, although we cannot—and should not be expected to—explain how it comes about that w's meaning *plus* is constituted by w's use being so-and-so, we might well be able to explain, by reference to a use-property it possesses, why w has the features on the basis of which it is recognized as meaning *plus*, and we could thereby justify the reduction of its meaning to that use-property.[11]

So I am left believing that the use of a predicate *does* determine (weakly) its extension, and does, therefore, determine (weakly) the infinitely many contexts to which it ought to be attributed.[12] There

[11] Christopher Peacocke, *A Study of Concepts* (Cambridge, Mass.: MIT Press, 1992), has developed an ingenious and sophisticated form of the use theory of meaning, whose general character is very much in tune with the view of meaning defended here. I must part company with him, however, when he maintains that the accounts of how concepts are constituted by their inferential roles must be supplemented by what he calls a 'determination theory'—a theory that would enable us to derive (i.e. read off) the referent of each term from the facts underlying its meaning. For it is precisely the main point of this paper to argue that there is no such theory, nor any need for one.

Consider a concept F whose identity is specified by a certain inferential role. The 'determination theory' in this case, Peacocke suggests, might be that *the referent of F is whatever would make the defining rules of inference come out valid.* But what I have been arguing here is, first, that such a theory is unnecessary since, once the concept F has been identified, its referent is specified disquotationally and trivially as the set of Fs; and second that the view that we need such a theory is motivated by an incorrect (inflationary) conception of truth and inference. A further objection, applicable to this particular determination theory, is that we simply have no reason to assume that concept-constituting rules of inference *must* be valid; what constitutes the concept is our *following* the rules, not their correctness.

[12] Granting that the use of a predicate does determine its extension—i.e. does determine to what we may truly apply it—I can imagine someone complaining that I had missed the real point of Kripke's argument. For isn't his real point that meaning has *normative* consequences—implying what one *ought* to say? Whereas a pattern of use, even if it does determine what it would be *true* to say, does not have intrinsic normative consequences.

The simple answer to this objection is that conditionals such as:

w means *DOG* → w is true of something iff it is a dog

appears to be no sense of 'determination' in which both of Kripke's premises are correct; and so his argument against the use-theory of meaning does not succeed.[13]

---

and

> w means DOG → one ought to apply w to something iff it is a dog

are on a par with one another in the following respect. Neither one constrains our analysis of the left-hand side. Rather, once we have found a satisfactory reductive analysis, $U(w)$, of 'w means DOG', then we can infer from that analysis, together with these conditionals, that

> $U(w)$ → w is true of something iff it is a dog

and

> $U(w)$ → one ought to apply w to something iff it is a dog

Thus the normative import of a certain regularity of word-use is no more difficult to accommodate than its truth-theoretic import.

[13] Kripke presents his sceptical considerations as raising the same problems for both *meaning* and *implicit rule following*, barely distinguishing between these two cases. Presumably he takes meaning to be a special case of implicit rule following, and infers that in so far as there are difficulties in identifying the facts in virtue of which a certain rule is being followed, the same difficulties must arise in identifying the facts in virtue of which a certain thing is meant by a word.

It seems to me, however, that the issue of which facts constitute our implicitly following the rule, 'Conform with regularity, R', does not have quite the same shape as the issue of meaning constitution. In addressing the former problem we can invoke the non-normative, purely naturalistic notion of 'ideal' that is widely deployed in the sciences—in speaking e.g. of the ideal gas laws, and ideally rigid bodies. We might suppose that a person's use of a word, w, is governed by a certain ideal law, $R(w)$. And it is then not unreasonable to think that this fact is what constitutes implicitly following the rule, 'Conform with $R(w)$'.

But this does not provide a solution to the problem of *meaning* constitution, as Kripke conceives of it. For, in light of his critique of dispositionalism, he ought to insist that our implicitly following a certain rule for a predicate's use can constitute its meaning only if it DETERMINES the word's extension. But surely no such DETERMINATION is possible unless the rule that is being implicitly followed is the one that dictates applying the predicate to exactly the objects within that extension? And it is very implausible that the rules of use of more than a few predicates have that character. Surely, our basic rule of use (if there is such thing) for 'electron' is not simply 'Apply "electron" to electrons and only electrons'. More plausibly, it will concern the evidential circumstances in which the word is to be deployed.

Needless to say, this does not prove that the theory is correct. There are many other serious and well-known objections to it. Exactly how are we to identify *which* of the regularities in a word's use constitutes its meaning? Can behaviourism and implausible forms of holism be avoided? Can compositionality be explained? What about meaningful sentences that are not used? What about words (like 'and' and 'but') with the same semantic content yet different uses? I am hopeful that these further challenges to the use-theory of meaning can be met; but if and how this may be done must remain to be seen.[A] What has been shown, I believe, is that the reduction of meaning to use is not put under any pressure whatsoever by the fact that words, in virtue of their meanings, are applied correctly to some things and incorrectly to others. For the problem in identifying which property underlies a given meaning is to find one that explains the behaviour—no matter whether correct or incorrect—on the basis of which that meaning is attributed. There is no need for this property to be one from which the correct applications can be 'read off'.

[A] For attempts to meet these challenges, amongst others, see my *Meaning* (1998).

5   On the Nature and Norms of Theoretical Commitment

1. Introduction

What is the right attitude to have towards a successful scientific theory? Some philosophers maintain that one is obliged to believe nothing beyond its *observable* implications. There can be no reason, they say, to give the slightest credence to any of its claims about the hidden, underlying reality. This epistemological position has been advocated in somewhat different forms by, for example, Hans Vaihinger, Pierre Duhem, Karl Popper, and recently Bas van Fraassen; and it is variously known as instrumentalism, fictionalism, theoretical scepticism, scientific anti-realism, constructive empiricism, and the philosophy of 'as if'.[1] Unlike certain other viewpoints

The first version of this paper was delivered to the Conference on Realism at Northwestern University in May, 1984. I would like to thank the participants in the subsequent discussion, and also Ned Block, Josh Cohen, and Marcus Giaquinto for their valuable comments and criticism.

[1] See H. Vaihinger, *The Philosophy of 'As If'; A System of the Theoretical, Practical and Religious Fictions of Mankind.* Reprint, tr C. K. Ogden (London: Routledge & Kegan Paul, 1949). Originally published as *Die Philosophie des Als-Ob* (Berlin: n.p., 1911); P. Duhem, *The Aim and Structure of Physical Theory.* Reprint, tr P. P. Wiener. (Princeton: Princeton University Press, 1954). Originally published as *La Théorie physique: Son objet, et sa structure* (Paris: Marcel Rivière & Cie 1906); K. Popper, *Conjectures and Refutations; The Growth of Scientific Knowledge* (New York: Basic Books, 1962); van B. Fraassen, *The Scientific Image.* (Oxford: Clarendon Press, 1980); 'Empiricism in the Philosophy of Science', in P. M. Churchland and C. A. Hooker (eds.), *Images of Science: Essays on Realism and Empiricism* (Chicago: University of Chicago Press, 1985, pp. 245–308).

that are also labelled 'anti-realistic', the idea to which I am referring is focused on the *justification* for theoretical belief, and does not directly concern meaning or metaphysics. It needn't deny that theories have content; that their postulates are true or false; nor does it call for an idiosyncratic understanding of the words 'true' and 'false'; and nor does it invoke analytic 'bridge' definitions in order to *identify* theories with purely observational commitments. Thus, its anti-realism is epistemological rather than reductionist, sceptical rather than semantic.[2] Corroborating data are said to support at most the conclusion that a theory will continue to work; they supposedly can give us no reason to believe its nonobservational content. On this sceptical basis, it is claimed that the proper aim of science is empirical adequacy rather than truth, and it is recommended that we merely *use* theories, believing their verifiable predictions but nothing more.

My intention here is to subject this point of view to a two-pronged attack. One component of the critique will be to oppose instrumentalism's ultimate recommendation. I will try to show, not just that one *should not* follow it, but that one *cannot*. This is because it presupposes a distinction between, on the one hand, *believing* a theory and, on the other hand, being disposed to use it, or, in van Fraassen's terminology, merely *accepting* it. But there is no such distinction, or so I will argue. Believing a theory is nothing over and above the mental state responsible for using it; and so the attitude urged by instrumentalism is impossible. That is the primary claim of this essay.

The other prong in my attack will be directed against the sceptical *basis* for the instrumentalist's recommendation. This further criticism is important. For even if his ultimate conclusion is incorrect for the reason just mentioned—that is, even if belief and

---

[2] For this reason, some philosophers might be inclined to deny that instrumentalism is, strictly speaking, a kind of anti-realism. This is a matter of terminology that has little bearing on the question at issue in this paper. For a discussion of the varieties of realism and their interaction with one another, see Essay 1.

acceptance are one and the same state of mind—that does not undermine the instrumentalist's main preliminary thesis, namely, that the inference from data to theory is always unreasonable. Therefore, he might well reformulate his position in one of two ways, to accommodate the identity of belief and acceptance. He might simply refuse to engage in theoretical science. Or he might concede that we ought indeed to believe theories given sufficient evidence, but maintain that our rationale in such a case could be at best pragmatic and to no extent epistemic. Because of these possible manoeuvres, a thoroughgoing refutation of instrumentalism cannot rest solely with a defence of theoretical belief. It must show in addition that such beliefs would be *epistemically* justified; or, in other words, that abductive reasoning (which goes from data to theory) is a valid form of nondeductive inference. I will therefore conclude this paper by scrutinizing some considerations that have been wrongly taken to demonstrate the invalidity of abduction: considerations having to do with 'onus of proof', 'underdetermination', and 'the sad fate of previous scientific theories'.

2. *Belief is the Same as Acceptance*

Let us focus on the usual situation in which we count ourselves lucky to have even a single theory at hand that captures all of our data in some domain. The instrumentalist doctrine recommends (or, at least, allows) that such a theory be just 'accepted' rather than believed. But this point of view presupposes that belief and acceptance are distinct attitudes, an assumption which is far from indubitable, though it is usually taken for granted.

In order to appreciate the problem here, bear in mind what it is to *accept* a theory, and then try to say what more would be involved in *believing* it. According to van Fraassen's characterization of the instrumentalist's posture, acceptance consists in believing just the observable consequences of a theory (including those observation statements that derive from the theory in conjunction with other accepted theories), and using the theory to make predictions, give explanations (without being committed to their truth), and design experiments. No wonder that Vaihinger called this the philosophy of 'as if'. For these are precisely the things that a believer would do. Yet it is suggested that we might accept our theories without believing them!

This is a distinction without a difference, or so I would like to argue. If we tried to formulate a psychological theory of the nature of belief, it would be plausible to treat beliefs as states with a particular kind of causal role. This would consist in such features as generating certain predications, prompting certain utterances, being caused by certain observations, entering in characteristic ways into inferential relations, playing a certain part in deliberation, and so on.[3] But that is to define belief in exactly the way instrumentalists characterize acceptance.

Thus, we have a prima-facie case for the thesis that belief simply *is* acceptance. Let me now bolster this case by trying to undercut the considerations that could tempt one to think that belief and acceptance are distinct attitudes. I have in mind four such considerations. The first is the idea that true believers believe they believe, whereas mere accepters of a theory do not. The second argument is based on the observation that even realists sometimes use a theory for practical purposes without believing it. In the third place, one might think that realism, unlike instrumentalism, involves a correspondence theory of truth. And fourth, it has been argued that a commitment to additional theoretical structure might increase the usefulness of a theory while decreasing its believability, implying that use and belief cannot be the same thing. Let me consider these points in turn.

BELIEVING THAT ONE BELIEVES

The differences between belief and acceptance, it might be claimed, is that believers *say*, or at least *think*, 'I believe this', whereas

---

[3] B. Loar, *Mind and Meaning* (Cambridge: Cambridge University Press, 1981).

mere accepters do not. However, facts of this sort hardly settle the matter. For it is perfectly plausible to maintain that such differences in behaviour are not the reflection of a difference between belief and acceptance but that they come, rather, from a difference between belief on the part of those who are not confused about their psychological states, and belief on the part of those who have been so muddled by philosophical double-talk that they are mistaken about the right way to describe their psychological state. In short, it is perfectly possible for someone to sincerely, yet mistakenly, deny her beliefs, that is, to believe without believing that she believes. So a difference between belief and acceptance is not implied merely by the possibility of conforming one's metabeliefs to instrumentalist doctrine.

Local Versus Global Instrumentalism

Another argument in favour of the instrumentalist's presupposition could proceed by reference to the familiar practice of treating at least *some* theories instrumentally. That is to say, even scientific realists will concede that, in certain circumstances, theories should be employed merely as heuristic devices for certain practical purposes but should not be taken, on a par with other theories, to be true. Consider such examples as the conservation of mass principle, the ideal gas laws, and Euclidean geometry. We can often base our expectations on these theories without believing them because we know that in the context at hand the extent of divergence from what will actually happen is not important. Thus, we understand perfectly well what being instrumentalists *some* of the time is like, and there should be no great leap of the imagination involved in comprehending a general form of instrumentalism.

The flaw in this line of thought is that the familiar local kind of instrumentalism that we undoubtedly *do* understand does not involve *all* the commitments characteristic of general philosophically motivated acceptance. The crucial difference is that general acceptance requires a belief in *all* of a theory's observational content and in *every* observation statement derivable by conjoining the theory with other accepted theories. On the other hand, when a theory is regarded instrumentally in normal scientific practice, it is always understood that its use is to be *confined* to a certain range of applications. It is understood that only predictions in a specified domain should be relied upon, and use of the theory in conjunction with other theories is also severely constrained. For example, we may suppose that a liquid is a continuous fluid for the purpose of designing a dam, but not in the context of studying Brownian motion. We can rely on Newtonian mechanics when dealing with slowly moving, medium-sized objects, but not necessarily otherwise. Thus, there is a crucial difference between the sort of acceptance involved in general, philosophical instrumentalism, and the attitude we have towards particular theories treated instrumentally for particular purposes. Consequently, our familiarity with qualified, local instrumentalism gives no reason to acknowledge the conceivability of unqualified, general instrumentalism.

Perhaps one could imagine a highly *radical* form of instrumentalism that would advocate a quite new scientific method in which the acceptance of theories would not require the acceptance of *all* their logical consequences and in which we would not aim for a unified view of the world but would be content with the piecemeal understanding provided by a set of minitheories that cannot be conjoined. This philosophy of science is easily distinguishable from realism, and easily distinguishable from actual scientific practice. However it is not what van Fraassen *et al.* are recommending.

It is worth noting, however, that their instrumentalism has been wrongly criticized out of a failure to distinguish it from this radical form of the doctrine. I have in mind the so-called 'conjunction objection'. The complaint (of e.g. Putnam and Boyd) is that an instrumentalist allegedly cannot accommodate the following aspect of scientific practice: if theories T_1 and T_2 are each successful, we tend to believe not merely the predictions of those theories taken individually, but also the observable consequences of their conjunction,

T_1 and T_2.[4] This practice could be explained by the fact that we come to believe that T_1 and T_2 are both true, and are then able to infer the truth of their conjunction. But it could not be explained if we restricted ourselves to the belief that T_1 and T_2 are each empirically adequate; for one cannot infer from this the empirical adequacy of T_1 and T_2.

So the objection goes; but it should not persuade. Suppose that T_1 and T_2 are individually the simplest theories[5] that fit the observed facts in domains D_1 and D_2 respectively, and that no other observations have been made that bear directly on their plausibility. The realists' principle is, roughly speaking:

Believe the simplest theory that fits the data.

However, this does not entitle them to conclude straightaway that we should believe T_1 and T_2. Their principle does not imply that each domain of observation justifies the simplest explanation of that domain. Rather, the idea is that we should believe the simplest *total* theory that accommodates *all* the data. Therefore, although T_1 and T_2 are individually simple and adequate to their special domains, they and their conjunction are credible only if they fit into the simplest overall account of the entire domain of observation, including D_1 and D_2. Happily, this condition is often satisfied, and that is why we often do make predictions based on the conjunction of separately supported theories.

Now, the (nonradical) instrumentalists can more or less parallel this explanation. They advocate the principle, roughly speaking:

Believe no more than the observable consequences of the simplest theory that fits the data.

---

[4] H. Putnam, *Meaning and the Moral Sciences* (London: Routledge & Kegan Paul, 1978); R. Boyd, 'Metaphor and Theory Change: What is "Metaphor" a Metaphor For?' in A. Ortony (ed.), *Metaphor and Thought* (Cambridge: Cambridge University Press, 1979, pp. 356–408).

[5] For the sake of conciseness and flexibility I am letting the term 'simplicity' stand, here and in what follows, for the entire range of putative theoretical virtues, which might include explanatory power, coherence, or beauty, that go beyond consistency and conformity with data.

But, like the realists, they must insist that this principle be construed holistically. Therefore, they want to know whether T_1 and T_2 will each be part of the simplest total theory. And if they think that each theory will be, then (and only then) may they conclude (like realists, but from their own weaker principle) that it is reasonable to believe the observable predictions of each theory and of their conjunction.

Thus instrumentalists and realists have equally good explanations of our tendency to conjoin separately confirmed theories and expect the combination to be empirically successful. As I have already said, this is not to preclude the possibility of a radical, revisionist brand of instrumentalism—overtly nonholistic—which could not, and would not wish to, accommodate our current practice. But that is not the doctrine under present discussion.

THE CORRESPONDENCE THEORY OF TRUTH

It might be objected that even if acceptance is a *form* of belief, still it does not constitute the sort of belief endorsed by realists. For realists, it might be said, hold that theories *correspond to reality* (whatever that means!); whereas instrumentalists, even if they, in some sense, 'believe' their theories, do not believe that they correspond to reality.

But this response simply changes the subject by exploiting the fact that philosophers mean various different things by the word 'realism'. The issue that we are concerned with here is whether one should, or should not, ever believe one's theories. This is the question of *scientific* (or epistemological) realism. A separate question is whether *truth* should be characterized as *correspondence with reality*. This might be called the issue of *metaphysical* realism.[A] I have been arguing that acceptance entails belief, and, thereby, have been trying to cast doubt on the possibility of a position opposed to

---

[A] I deploy this terminology in Essay 1; but indicate in its footnote E the reasons for which I came to abandon it.

scientific realism. Therefore, in responding to this argument, it is irrelevant to point out that acceptance does not entail endorsement of a correspondence theory of truth and so does not entail metaphysical realism. Scientific realists may well confine themselves to the claim that theories are sometimes credible; and they need not, and in my view should not, go beyond some version of the redundancy conception of truth.[6]

THEORETICAL UNIFICATION

Finally, we should consider an argument for the distinctness of belief and instrumental acceptance that has been suggested by van Fraassen. Suppose a new, deep theory is proposed that unifies and explains various more superficial generalizations. This increase in degree of unity would *increase the acceptability* of our overall theory, making it simpler and, therefore, more useful. However, it *decreases the believability* of our theory since additional claims are now involved, and so it is now more likely that the theory will go wrong somewhere, In other words, belief and acceptance should respond differently to theoretical unification, and so cannot be the same thing.

My quarrel with this reasoning is that, contrary to first appearances, no property has in fact been specified that applies to belief but not to acceptance, or vice versa. Beliefs are subject to various forms of evaluation. They are commonly appraised with respect to *epistemic* norms and are judged appropriate or not in relation to the available evidence. In addition we sometimes consider the *pragmatic* value of having certain beliefs. It is in this practical sense that, according to Pascal, one ought to believe in God. Now, as van Fraassen says, an effect of theoretical unification is to decrease the credibility of our total theory, but this observation relates solely to *epistemic* rationality. From the perspective of practical concerns we

---

[6] For an extended defence of this view see P.G. Horwich, *Truth* (Oxford: Blackwell, 1990)—2nd edn., 1998.

have *more* reason to believe the unified theory. Thus (as in the case of Pascal's wager) a tension exists between the dictates of epistemic and practical reason with regard to what we should believe. The same goes for acceptance, or so I would argue. Van Fraassen correctly maintains that unification will yield a total theory that we have more reason to accept since it will be more desirable from the practical standpoint. In addition, if belief and acceptance are indeed identical, then in the epistemic sense, there will be *less* reason to accept the unified theory. Thus belief and acceptance will respond in the same way to theoretical unification. Now, one could deny this. One could insist that considerations of abductive epistemic rationality do not apply to the mental state of acceptance, but this response would beg the question. It would simply presuppose that belief and acceptance are distinct states, and provide neither an argument for their distinctness nor a response to our grounds for scepticism on this point. In short, the difference between epistemic and pragmatic norms of evaluation does not entail a corresponding difference between states of mind to be evaluated.

These four points and replies do not of course *establish* the identity of belief and acceptance, but they suggest that such a view has a lot to be said for it. And if it is true, then full conformity with instrumentalism is not even *conceivable*, let alone rational.

To be completely fair, we should note that, in certain formulations, scientific realism would be equally susceptible to this criticism. Consider a realist who claims that when a theory is well-corroborated, one should not only use it, but *also* believe it. Such a realist is guilty of the same dubious presupposition: that belief transcends acceptance. Thus, we might think of the point, not as an argument against instrumentalism, but rather as the removal of a misconception shared by both realists and instrumentalists, one which has fuelled the conflict between them. Having said this, however, I suspect, nonetheless, that many more realists than instrumentalists will derive comfort from the fact that belief does not transcend acceptance.

This is because the most common way of characterizing the dispute is 'whether to believe or not to believe'; and our conclusion purports to eliminate the second of these options.

Although I have been addressing explicitly the traditional brand of scientific instrumentalism articulated in the twentieth century by Vaihinger, Duhem, Popper, and van Fraassen, the present conclusion would seem to have similar implications for some other instances of epistemological anti-realism. I cannot elaborate these here; but I have in mind two recent examples. First, there is Nancy Cartwright's *mild* instrumentalism.[7] She is prepared to grant the credibility of nonobservable, phenomenological laws; but she embraces instrumentalism with respect to very general theoretical laws. Second, there is Hartry Field's nominalism.[8] He urges scepticism with respect to the existence of mathematical entities. Nevertheless, he holds that it is fine to *use* mathematics, since reference to numbers and their properties is a dispensable conservative extension of logical facts whose credibility is not so problematic. In both of these cases, our conclusion tends to suggest that the purported disbelief would be belied in practice.[B]

3. *Onus of Proof*

As I mentioned at the outset, even if belief and acceptance are the same thing, this does not mean that realism and instrumentalism must collapse into one another. For there remains the following difference between them. Realists grant the legitimacy of abductive inference, so

[7] *How the Laws of Physics Lie* (Oxford: Clarendon Press, 1983).

[8] *Science Without Numbers: A Defence of Nominalism* (Princeton: Princeton University Press, 1982).

[B] A couple of other domains in which instrumentalism/fictionalism has been advocated are ethical discourse (e.g. Daniel Nolan, Greg Restall, and Caroline West, 'Moral Fictionalism', unpublished) and possible world discourse (e.g. Gideon Rosen, 'Modal Fictionalism', *Mind*, 99/395 (1990), 327–54. The present line of thought would suggest that neither of these positions is tenable.

they think that there are good epistemic reasons (as well as pragmatic reasons) for theoretical belief. Instrumentalists, on the other hand, deny that abductive inference is guaranted. Therefore, while they concede that theoretical belief is desirable, they hold that the justification for it is purely pragmatic. This second part of the paper addresses some considerations that have been adduced in favour of scepticism about abductive inference and discusses what is wrong with them.

In the first place, there is a tendency to think that realism, since it involves the commitment to an *additional* form of inference, bears the onus of proof, and therefore that a case for scepticism can be made simply by listing and rebutting all of the prorealist arguments that have been proposed so far. For example, van Fraassen gives no arguments against realism in his book, *The Scientific Image*. He simply subjects various weak arguments in favour of realism to devastating criticism.[9]

---

[9] The most popular argument for realism, the 'miracle argument' (see e.g. J. J. C. Smart, *Between Science and Philosophy* (New York: Random House, 1968: 150); Putnam: 18–19) is simply that it would be an incredibly unlikely coincidence—a miracle—for all the empirical consequences of a theory to be true, and yet the theory itself not to be true. But, as an attempted refutation of theoretical scepticism, this reasoning is plainly inadequate since it blatantly begs the question. The (thoughtful) instrumentalists' position is, unabashedly, that it is *not* improbable for a theory to be false while its empirical consequences are true. Moreover, whether this eventuality would qualify as a 'miracle' depends on how rare an occurrence it would be. According to instrumentalists, we are in no position to suppose that there would be anything unusual (or 'miraculous') about such a thing. After all, he says, we have no way of establishing that this is not *always* the situation. Nor is the miracle argument improved by shifting emphasis to the fact that *scientific methodology yields successful theories* (R. Boyd, 'Scientific Realism and Naturalistic Epistemology', in P. D. Asquith and R. N. Giere (eds.), *PSA 1980*, ii. East Lansing (Philosophy of Science Association, 1981, pp. 613–62). Whether it is indeed miraculously improbable for this to be so without it also being the case that scientific methodology yields *true* theories is just as doubtful for instrumentalists, and for the same reason, as the thesis that the theories themselves are not likely to be successful unless they are true. See A. Fine, 'The Natural Ontological Attitude', In J. Leplin (ed.), *Scientific Realism*. Berkeley and Los Angeles (University of California Press, 1984, pp. 83–107) for a good critique of miracle arguments.

Admittedly, the attitude that the onus of proof is on the side of realism does have a certain initial plausibility. Notice that we are not now referring to realists' obligation to provide some grounds for their theoretical claims, an obligation which they concede and regard themselves as discharging by reference to data, simplicity, and so on; but, rather, the idea that realists are also under an obligation to show that such considerations are adequate. I suspect that the pull of this idea derives from something like the following principle:

> (J) A belief is required only in so far as the method of inference used to obtain it has been given external support

in which 'external support' involves some sort of explicit, justifying argument. On that assumption, the absence of any explicit reason to suppose that observational data confirm theoretical conclusions will entail that theoretical beliefs cannot be justified, and therefore that they need not be adopted.

However, it seems clear that this line of thought, in particular, principle J, is mistaken. Note, in the first place, that we do not always insist that correct normative claims must have been given external support. For example, we are morally required to tell the truth, avoid harming people, and so on; yet, no one would suggest that, in the absence of external support, we should not feel bound by such ethical rules. Secondly, and more to the point, justifying simple *inductive* inferences is notoriously difficult and perhaps impossible. Nonetheless, anyone who violates our inductive practice (anyone, for example, who insists that experience offers no good reason to accept that humans cannot fly unaided from tall buildings) is reckoned to be irrational.

Considerations such as these might well diminish our attachment to principle J. The main argument against it, however, is that its fulfilment is logically impossible. If every legitimate rule of inference were to require a basis of explicit, external support, then we would be required, on top of providing that support, to justify whatever reasoning is employed to get from the needed basis of external support to the rule of inference in question. But *that* justification would then itself stand in need of support. And so on. We are drawn into either an infinite regress or a circle of which neither is capable of providing a basis of external support. Now, presumably we are not going to accept that *all* our inferences are bad ones. Therefore, we must conclude that *J* is too strict a requirement.

To endorse this conclusion is merely to accept that 'the chain of reasons must come to an end', which is hardly controversial. I don't want to imply either that instrumentalists typically fail to recognize this point, or that the only way for them to put the burden of proof onto realism is by brandishing principle *J*. An alternative way is to acknowledge that *certain* things may be legitimately assumed without explicit support, while maintaining that the inferential rules in question are not among this privileged set of basic principles. But even if this claim is true, it is surely not obviously true. And so, if we are to become convinced of its truth, then some sort of argument is called for.

Thus, given that chains of justification must terminate, our practice of reasoning from observation to theory might be sound even if we cannot explicitly show it to be sound. Instrumentalism asserts that it is *not* sound. However, this thesis can claim our allegiance only by means of an argument that must do one of two things: either demonstrate the invalidity of such inferences, or show that they do not belong in the category of practices that are acceptable in the absence of explicit support.

4. Underdetermination

An argument of the first type is not hard to find. Though not always explicit, I think that the lurking rationale for theoretical scepticism is a conviction that the hidden truth is *underdetermined* by the possible data—that there is bound to be more than one way to explain the set of observable facts. This view is not merely a *possible* route to instrumentalism, but the *only* way to get there; for to doubt a theory is to suspect that some other theory might be true instead. (Even the claim that there are *no* unobservable entities is still a theoretical claim.) Suppose that some potentially troublesome alternative were *not* empirically equivalent to our theory. The recognition of its possible truth would then have consequences more radical than are demanded by instrumentalism: it would entail doubts about the *observable* predictions of our theory. Thus, it must be that instrumentalism is the product of a concern about empirically equivalent alternatives.[10]

This is not to say that the prospect of underdetermination is, in itself, a sufficient basis for theoretical scepticism; for a realist can accept this possibility yet contend that there are relevant differences in simplicity[11]—and, hence, in intrinsic plausibility—among empirically equivalent total theories. Therefore, instrumentalists

[10] A frequently expressed objection to instrumentalism is that it presupposes a dubious distinction between observable and theoretical phenomena. I have two reasons for not relying on this criticism. In the first place, despite the widespread scepticism regarding the existence of such a distinction, there is still something to be said for the view that some version of it is psychologically real, and epistemologically important, and can be adequately characterized. See e.g. W. V. Quine, 'Empirical Content', in *Theories and Things* (Cambridge, Mass.: Belknap Press of Harvard University Press, 1981, pp. 24–30). In the second place, even if the standard critique of the observation/theory distinction is correct, it touches only certain formulations of instrumentalism and does not go to the heart of the matter. For there would nonetheless be a distinction, given a conflict among various theoretical systems, between the realm of claims that, all sides can agree, may be decided independently of which of the theories one is in sympathy with and the 'theoretical' claims that are tested in light of their capacity to explain these contextually neutral facts. Thus abductive inference is still called for. If it is invalid, as instrumentalists say, then the thesis that observation is theory-laden—the renunciation of absolutely neutral data—merely increases the scope of his sceptical conclusion, and certainly does nothing to undermine it.

[11] Note that I continue to use the term 'simplicity' as short for a broad range of putative theoretical virtues, not just simplicity.

must not only embrace underdetermination; they must argue, in addition, for at least one of the following positions:

(1) There is no reason to suppose that, other things being equal, simpler theories are more plausible than more complex ones;

or

(2) We have to worry about alternative total theories that are just as simple as ours.

The first of these strategies raises, once again, the issue of 'onus of proof' discussed in the last section. For the mere fact (if it is a fact) that no one has (or could) come up with an argument for the evidential relevance of simplicity does not constitute a reason for doubting its relevance. The case for instrumentalism requires positive grounds for maintaining that simplicity is not an indicator of truth.

Now, there is one argument that is sometimes supposed to suffice. I have in mind a line of reasoning that Putnam has called 'the disastrous meta-induction': namely, that the usual canons of theory choice, which incorporate our preference for simplicity, constantly lead us to theories that turn out wrong; therefore, these inferential principles have been refuted by the history of science and we should have no confidence in them.

I cannot here give this argument the detailed criticism that it deserves (but see my *Probability and Evidence*). Suffice it to say that, although many of our theoretical beliefs have indeed been mistaken, one must not overlook the fact that a good number of long-standing scientific discoveries still look highly plausible. Consider our belief that the sun is just one among millions of other stars, that the species of living things evolved through natural selection, and that diamonds and charcoal are different forms of the same stuff. Despite the 'disastrous meta-induction', we think it unlikely that these ideas will be overthrown. Such examples suggest that the history of science should serve merely as a warning against overconfidence. Depending on the quality of the evidence, our theoretical beliefs should be more or less tentative and uncertain; but there is no need to overreact by renouncing them altogether.

Thus, it is far from clear how one might justify the sceptical thesis that simplicity is no sign of truth. Let us turn, then, to the other imagined basis for instrumentalism. Suppose that the evidential significance of simplicity is granted. Scepticism may nonetheless seem appropriate, given the prospect of *simple* alternatives to our total conception of the world. For why should we believe our theory, if there is a competitor that is equally plausible?

To see what is wrong with this reasoning, notice the distinction between claiming that there *is* such an alternative, and claiming that there *might be* one. The first thesis would indeed constitute a prima facie case for scepticism. But there is, in general, no ground for thinking it true. After all, finding *one* simple theory that fits all the observed facts, let alone *two*, is difficult. The second thesis is admittedly plausible. We perhaps cannot *prove* that there is no simple rival of our theory, but this does not justify scepticism since the probability that there actually *is* such an alternative is very small.

I have claimed that, even if the existence of underdetermination is conceded, then one of two further things remains to be shown if one is to have reason to renounce inference from data to theory. Neither of those things has ever been done, as far as I know. However, I don't mean to suggest that the existence of underdetermination can be taken for granted. Far from it. Even this first step in the case for instrumentalism is by no means evident or noncontroversial. To appreciate the problem here, keep in mind the difference between a *theory* and a *theory-formulation*. It is indeed noncontroversial that, given our total theory-formulation, S_1, there will always be an alternative, S_2, containing the same observation sentences. (As a trivial example, consider the formulation that would be generated from a typical expression of our scientific beliefs, by interchanging the words 'electron' and 'atom'.) But alternative formulations need not confront us with a choice of theories, because we might hold that the use of S_2, rather than our current S_1, would amount merely to the adoption of a new language, that is, a different way of expressing our old beliefs, rather than the adoption of a new theory. That interpretation of the situation is intuitively plausible in the 'electron'/'atom' example; and it is not at all obvious that there are *any* cases of alternative, empirically equivalent formulations that could not be reconciled in this way.[12]

5. *Conclusion*

I have tried to undermine two forms of instrumentalism: a stronger and a weaker version. According to the strong version, abductive inference is invalid and so it is legitimate to renounce theoretical belief. Against this I argued that there is no difference between believing a theory and being disposed to use it; therefore the instrumentalists' proposal is incoherent. But this leaves open a weaker form of instrumentalism, namely, that since abductive inference is invalid, the justification for theoretical belief can be nothing more than pragmatic. Against this I suggested that, contrary to initial appearances, the onus is with the instrumentalist to show that abductive inference is invalid, rather than with the realist to prove its validity. To that end, the only possible strategy is to argue on the basis of underdetermination. Considerable difficulties, however,

---

[12] Putnam's 'model theoretic' argument (1978) suggests that the choice among empirically equivalent alternatives is always a matter of convention—a decision between languages, not theories. I try to develop this point of view in Essay 3 and in 'A Defence of Conventionalism', in G. MacDonald and C. Wright (eds.), *Fact, Science and Morality: Essays on A. J. Ayer's* Language, Truth, and Logic (New York: Blackwell, 1986, pp. 163–87).

have emerged: first, that the very existence of underdetermination may reasonably be called into question; second, that even if under-determination is present, it does not alone suffice for the sceptical conclusion; and third, that the necessary additional assumptions are very far from having been made plausible.

6 Wittgensteinian Bayesianism

Belief is not an all-or-nothing matter. Rather, there are various *degrees* of conviction which may be represented by numbers between zero and one. Were we ideally rational, our full beliefs (of degree one) would comply with the laws of deductive logic; they would be consistent and closed under logical implication. And similarly, our *degrees* of belief should conform to the probability calculus (including an important theorem proved by Thomas Bayes).[1] This enrichment of epistemology—provided by the addition of degrees of belief and an appreciation of their probabilistic 'logic'—fosters progress with respect to many problems in the philosophy of science.

These statements form the core of a programme, which I will call 'therapeutic Bayesianism', whose primary goal is the solution of various puzzles and paradoxes that come from reflecting on scientific methods. Its creed is that many of these problems are the product of oversimplification, and that the above-mentioned elementary probabilistic model of degrees of belief often contains just the right balance of accuracy and simplicity to enable us to command a clear

I have greatly benefited from James Woodward's thorough and perceptive criticism. I would also like to thank Ned Block, Susan Brison, Josh Cohen, Marcus Giaquinto, Mark Kaplan, and Judith Thomson for helping me to improve earlier drafts of this paper.

[1] The axioms of elementary probability theory are as follows: (1) probabilities are less than or equal to one; (2) the probability of a logical truth is equal to one; (3) if two statements are jointly impossible, then the probability that at least one of them is true is equal to the sum of their individual probabilities; and (4) the conditional probability of p given q equals the probability of the conjunction of p and q divided by the probability of q.

view of the issues and see where we were going wrong.[2] This somewhat Wittgensteinian goal and creed distinguishes therapeutic Bayesianism from more systematic enterprises in which probabilistic degrees of belief play a prominent role: for example, Bayesian decision theory, Bayesian statistics, Bayesian psychology, Bayesian semantics, and Bayesian history of science. It is especially important to appreciate the difference between the paradox resolving orientation of therapeutic Bayesianism—that of exploiting a simple, idealized model in order to help illuminate notorious philosophical perplexities—and the quite distinct project of providing a perfectly true and complete (descriptive or normative) *theory* of scientific practice. The latter task might well involve the postulation of belief-gradations, and might also be done in the name of philosophy of science. However, its aims are quite different; and one must beware of judging one project by adequacy conditions appropriate to the other.[3]

Therapeutic Bayesianism is not self-evidently beneficial, but it does have some prima-facie plausibility. Moreover, this plausibility is enhanced by substantial accomplishments, and, as we shall see, a great deal of the criticism it has received is misdirected—commonly for the reason just indicated. In this paper I would like to try to make a case for the programme by discussing it from three, progressively

[2] This project is attempted in my *Probability and Evidence* (Cambridge: Cambridge University Press, 1982), henceforth abbreviated as *P&E*. The metaphilosophical outlook is inspired by Wittgenstein's *Philosophical Investigations*, §§ 88–133.

[3] Bayesian programmes of various kinds have been developed in the work of Rudolf Carnap, David Christensen, R. T. Cox, Bruno de Finetti, Ron Giere, I. J. Good, John Earman, Ellery Eells, Hartry Field, Allan Franklin, Ian Hacking, Mary Hesse, Jaakko Hintikka, Colin Howson, E. T. Jaynes, Richard Jeffrey, Harold Jeffreys, Mark Kaplan, J. M. Keynes, Henry Kyburg, Isaac Levi, Patrick Maher, Roger Rosencrantz, Wesley Salmon, L. J. Savage, Teddy Seidenfeld, Abner Shimony, Brian Skyrms, Patrick Suppes, Peter Urbach, Bas van Fraassen, and others. Much of this work (especially the studies by Good, Hesse, Howson and Urbach, and Earman) contains contributions to therapeutic Bayesianism. However, I cannot attribute to these philosophers the project that I have in mind by that label, since their work is oriented towards the discovery of a 'theory of science', and thus reflects a metaphilosophical point of view that is quite distinct from that of the programme which I am calling 'therapeutic Bayesianism'.

abstract, points of view: substantial, foundational, and metaphilosophical. More specifically, there will follow sections on: (1) 'The Fruitfulness of Therapeutic Bayesianism', in which I will sketch treatments of the 'raven' paradox and the puzzle of diverse data, and go on to mention various other applications; (2) 'Probabilistic Foundations', in which the propriety of certain idealizations will be defended—particularly the representation of belief by numbers, the adoption of probabilistic canons of reason governing such beliefs, the definition of confirmation as increase in rational degree of belief, and the idea that induction may be codified in a confirmation function; and (3) 'Misplaced Scientism', in which I criticize a meta-philosophical perspective that does not properly distinguish science from the philosophy of science, and which overvalues the use of symbolic apparatus. Along the way, I shall respond to some criticisms of therapeutic Bayesianism that have recently been advanced.

1. The Fruitfulness of Therapeutic Bayesianism

A good illustration of therapeutic Bayesianism at work is its way of treating the notorious 'raven paradox'. It is plausible to suppose that any hypothesis of the form 'All Fs are G' would be supported by the observation of an F that is also G. But if this is generally true, then the discovery of a non-black non-raven (e.g. a white shoe) confirms that all non-black things are non-ravens; and thereby confirms the logically equivalent hypothesis, 'All ravens are black'—a seemingly bizarre conclusion. This is 'the paradox of confirmation'. The Bayesian approach to this problem is to argue that observing a known raven to be black will *substantially* confirm 'All ravens are black', whereas observing that a known non-black thing is not a raven will confirm it only *negligibly*—the difference being explained, roughly speaking, by the fact that, given our background beliefs about the chances of coming across ravens and black things, the first of these observations is more surprising, more of a test of the hypothesis, and therefore more evidentially powerful, than the second. Thus, the paradoxical flavor of our conclusion comes from the not unnatural confusion of negligible support with no support at all—a confusion sustained by inattention to degrees of belief and their bearing on confirmation.

A formal version of this analysis proceeds from the following premises:

(a) That the amount of support for hypothesis H provided by evidence E is the factor by which the rational degree of belief in H is enhanced by the discovery of E—which is indicated by the ratio of subjective probabilities, P(H/E)/P(H), for a rational person.

(b) That a rational person's degrees of belief will ideally conform to the probability calculus; and, in particular, will obey Bayes's Theorem:

$$\frac{P(H/E)}{P(H)} = \frac{P(E/H)}{P(E)}$$

(To appreciate the intuitive plausibility of this theorem, note that it derives from the fact that the conditional probability of H given E is equal to the probability of the conjunction of H and E, divided by the probability of E: i.e. P(H/E) = P(H&E)/P(E). See Figure 3.

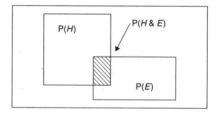

Figure 3

Therefore, since P(H&E) = P(E&H), we obtain P(H/E)P(E) = P(E/H)P(H), and hence Bayes's Theorem).

(c) That our degree of belief (prior to the investigation, and given the known scarcity of ravens) that a randomly selected non-black thing would turn out to be a non-raven is high.

(d) That our prior degree of belief (prior to the investigation, and given the known abundance of non-black things) that a randomly selected raven would turn out not to be black is substantial.

Now let us compare the support for the hypothesis, H, that all ravens are black, provided, first, by the discovery concerning a known raven that it is black (which is symbolized as $R^* B$), and, second, by the discovery that a known non-black thing is not a raven $(-B^* -R)$. Applying premise (a) and then (b), we find:

$$\text{Support provided by } (R^* B) = \frac{P(H/R^* B)}{p(H)} = \frac{P(R^* B/H)}{P(R^* B)}$$

Support provided by $(-B^* -R)$

$$= \frac{P(H/-B^* -R)}{p(H)} = \frac{P(-B^* -R/H)}{P(-B^* -R)}$$

But our hypothesis *entails* that any known raven would be black and any known non-black thing would not be a raven; therefore, $P(R^* B/H) = 1$ and $P(-B^* -R/H) = 1$. Therefore

Support from raven found to be black	$= \dfrac{P(H/R^* B)}{P(H)} = \dfrac{1}{P(R^* B)} =$	1/prior degree of belief that a known raven would be black
Support from non-black thing found not to be a raven	$= \dfrac{P(H/-B^* -R)}{P(H)} = \dfrac{1}{P(-B^* -R)} =$	1/prior degree of belief that a known non-black thing would not be a raven

Now one may assume (premise (c)) that a normal investigator of the hypothesis has prior background knowledge about the rough distribution of ravens and black things in his vicinity, and that this will lead him to expect that there is a very good chance that a randomly selected non-black thing will turn out not to be a raven.

Thus $P(-B^* \, -R)$ is very nearly 1; and the amount of support for the hypothesis provided by observing that a non-black thing is not a raven is very little.

On the other hand, we would expect the background of investigation to dictate, in addition, (premise (d)) that the likelihood of a randomly selected raven being black is not especially high. After all, as far as we know at the outset of the research, there are many colours that the raven could perfectly well have. Thus $P(R^* \, B)$ is a good deal less than one. Therefore, the amount of support provided by observing that a known raven is black is substantial.

One might object to this reasoning that the final assumption is false, since the *objective* chances of finding that a raven is black are actually extremely high. However, this objection is based on a slip which is easy to identify. It confuses 'probability' in the sense of *subjective degree of belief* and 'probability' in the sense of *relative frequency*. All the probabilities mentioned in the argument are rational subjective probabilities, and it is under that construal that we may reasonably assume that $P(R^* \, B)$ is not near to 1. The feeling that this assumption is wrong derives from incorrectly reading $P(R^* \, B)$ as a relative frequency assertion. In that sense, since in fact almost all ravens are black, the probability that a randomly selected raven will be black is indeed very great. But this fact has no bearing on the argument.[4]

---

[4] Stephen Spielman's objection is based on the mistake described here: the identification of the probabilities with objective proportions. (See his review of *P&E*, *Journal of Philosophy* (Mar. 1984), 168–73. Page references for Spielman are to this work.)

To keep things relatively simple I have assumed that there are just *two* observations in question: namely, the discovery regarding a randomly selected raven that it is black and the discovery regarding a randomly selected non-black thing that it is not a raven. If we consider instead the discovery that a known black thing is a raven, or various other ways of seeing black ravens and non-black non-ravens, then the existence of confirmation will depend on the presence of special additional background assumptions (e.g. that ravens are quite likely all to have the same colour). Nonetheless a similar contrast between the degrees of confirmation provided by black ravens and non-black non-ravens may be established. In *P&E* I suggest that these other ways of seeing black ravens would provide *no* confirmation of the hypothesis.

A similar objection is to deny that there could be any difference in evidential import between identifying a known raven as black and identifying a known black thing as a raven. Howson and Urbach,[5] for example, maintain that the only difference between these two data is the time order in which the elements of the observed fact are established. They think that in each case what is eventually known is the same, so there can be no variation in confirmation power between the two discoveries. Imagine, however, that an ornithologist instructs her assistant to go and find a black raven and bring it back to the lab for inspection; obviously, that inspection would count for nothing. But there is no paradox here, even though we might loosely speak of 'seeing a black raven' in all three cases. For a more precise character-ization of the evidence shows that what is discovered in each case is not really the same. That a randomly selected raven turns out to be black, that a randomly selected black thing turns out to be a raven and that a randomly selected black raven turns out to be a black raven, are very different pieces of information, and it should not be surprising that they confirm our hypothesis to different degrees.

Therapeutic Bayesianism handles other issues in the philosophy of science similarly, putting a lot of weight on premises (a) and (b).

This is misleading. Sometimes our background theories include a belief in the projectibility of the generalization in question, and in that case all the ways of observing an instance of it will normally provide confirmation.

My treatment of the paradox is, in a couple of respects, different from Patrick Suppes's analysis: 'A Bayesian Approach to the Paradoxes of Confirmation', in J. Hintikka and P. Suppes (eds.), *Aspects of Inductive Logic* (Amsterdam: North Holland, 1966). In the first place, he does not distinguish between the discovery that a randomly selected object is a black raven and the discovery that a randomly selected raven is black; whereas it is a significant feature of my account that in certain circumstances only the latter datum would confirm the hypothesis. And secondly, he does not obtain his results from the basic principles of Bayesianism— the thesis that degrees of belief should conform to the probability calculus; rather, he starts with the assumption that surprising observations have greater confirmation power; and this, though correct, is much better derived than simply presupposed.

[5] C. Howson and P. Urbach, *Scientific Reasoning: The Bayesian Approach* (La Salle, Ill.; Open Court, 1989).

By combining the idea of confirmation as enhancement of rational degree of belief with the principle that rational degrees of belief should satisfy the probability calculus, we get a way of treating those problems that hinge upon considerations having to do with *degree of support*. Therefore the method has a wide scope. In particular, one can expect to shed light on why 'surprising' predictions have relatively great confirmation power, what is wrong with *ad hoc* hypotheses, whether prediction has more evidential value than mere accommodation of data, why a diverse collection of consonant facts can confirm a theory more than a narrow data set, why we base our judgements on as much data as possible, how statistical hypotheses can be testable despite their unfalsifiability, what is peculiar about 'grue-like' hypotheses, and various other problems.

These issues are unified by their involvement with the notion of 'varying evidential quality'; and this is why traditional epistemology, with its fixation on all-or-nothing belief, is not able to resolve them. It is only to be expected that the introduction of degrees of belief, together with an understanding of the rational constraints to which they are subject, would open the way to progress. Of course, there is not the space here to fully substantiate this thesis by describing all these applications of therapeutic Bayesianism. Let me, however, give one further illustration of the approach.

Consider the hypothesis (the Wiedermann–Franz Law) that the electrical conductivity of a metal is proportional to its thermal conductivity. This would be supported somewhat by 100 paired measurements of electrical with thermal conductivity, all consonant with the hypothesis, of which 50 are performed on samples of sodium and 50 on samples of zinc, and where the mass and shape of the samples are varied. But the hypothesis would be more strongly confirmed by 100 consonant measurements if ten rather than merely two different metals were examined, and if the temperatures of the sample were varied within each group. Why is this? In general, how is it that a broad spectrum of different kinds of fact, when entailed by a hypothesis, will confirm it to a greater degree than a uniform, repetitive set of data? It is natural to answer as follows. To the extent that our observations cover a broad range of phenomena, they are capable of falsifying a large number of alternative hypotheses, which then bequeath substantial credibility to those hypotheses that survive. Now, this solution does not quite work. For a narrow data set can preclude just as *many* hypotheses as a diverse data set. Nevertheless, we can repair the solution by noting that there is a significant difference in the *kinds* of hypotheses that are excluded by the two sets of facts. We should notice that the diverse data tend to exclude more of the *simple* alternative hypotheses than do the narrow data. Given a representation of simplicity in terms of high prior probability,[6] this suggests that diverse data tend to rule out more high-probability alternatives than narrow data. But if so, then a hypothesis that survives relatively diverse observations becomes more probable than one that is left in the running by a narrow set of data.

Figure 4 provides another illustration. The data set E(narrow) excludes (given experimental error) just as many alternatives to the line H(straight) as does E(diverse). Nonetheless E(diverse) confirms H(straight) more strongly than E(narrow) does, because E(diverse) is better than E(narrow) at excluding simple alternatives to H(straight)—for example, gradual curves—which have an initially high probability. Thus H(gradual) is ruled out by E(diverse) but not by E(narrow). On the other hand, the sort of hypothesis, like H(crazy), prohibited by E(narrow) yet not by E(diverse), is not very probable anyway; so excluding it does not greatly benefit those hypotheses that survive. Thus, with the help of a probabilistic representation of simplicity, we can begin to account for our methodological intuitions concerning diverse data.[7]

---

[6] An argument for associating simplicity with high prior probability is given in *P&E*, 70–1.

[7] Teddy Seidenfeld maintains that this account goes in the 'wrong direction'. But he gives no grounds for that claim other than to note deficiencies in our understanding of simplicity—our inability to solve either the descriptive or the normative

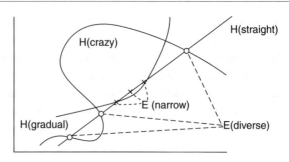

Figure 4

2. *Probabilistic Foundations*

In the last section I have tried to indicate something of the fruitfulness of therapeutic Bayesianism. Let me now consider various foundational questions that might be thought to cast doubt on the project:

1. Do people actually have numerical degrees of belief?
2. If so, can it be shown that *rational* degrees of belief must conform to the probability calculus?
3. Is it correct to identify degree of confirmation with rational enhancement of subjective probability?
4. Are there objective facts of confirmation?
5. Does reason require *merely* that one's beliefs conform to the probability calculus? Or is it the case (as Carnap thought) that a rational system of beliefs is subject to several further constraints?
6. If further constraints are needed, then what are they?

On the first question, perhaps we should be agnostic. The successes of therapeutic Bayesianism will reinforce the evident fact that its

---

problems surrounding it. And it seems to me that his observation is irrelevant in the absence of any reason to believe either (*a*) that we can get a satisfactory explication of simplicity in terms of evidential diversity, or (*b*) that the Bayesian account would not withstand a better grasp of simplicity. (See his review of *P&E, Philosophical Review* (July 1984).)

basic principles are at least *roughly* correct. Thus we know that there are belief gradations of some sort, that there are rational constraints governing them (prohibiting, for example, a high degree of confidence in two contradictory propositions), and that confirmation is not wholly unrelated to increasing belief. Moreover, the Bayesian representation of these ideas has a great deal of plausibility. Consider a spectrum of situations in which we know that the propensities (as manifested by relative frequencies) of certain events are $x_1, x_2, \ldots, x_N$. For each such case there is a corresponding epistemic attitude—a degree of confidence—that the next trial will produce an event of the designated type. Presumably the appropriate attitude will vary with the relative frequency. Specifically, since the frequencies range over numbers between zero and one, so will the degrees of confidence.

However, despite the attractiveness of such considerations, one must of course acknowledge that the Bayesian framework might be wrong. The crude ideas that it represents should not be controversial. However, it is quite possible that the Bayesian articulation of those ideas is not absolutely right; and that, in particular, the assumption of precise-valued, numerical degrees of belief is incorrect.

Even so, such a model could be an excellent idealization, sufficing perfectly well for the primary purposes of therapeutic Bayesianism: namely, to dispel confusion, resolve problems, and thereby improve our understanding of the scientific method. For the paradoxes are caused by forgetting the *crude* facts (that there are gradations of belief, etc.) or by failing to recognize their significance. And so the solutions will involve noticing that those rough ideas have been overlooked and coming to appreciate how they bear on the problems. This sort of treatment will not depend essentially on any particular theoretical refinements. The function of the Bayesian framework is merely to cast the crude, uncontroversial ideas into a form where their impact on our problems can have maximal clarity and force.

What then is the import of studies that cast doubt on the existence of numerical degrees of conviction and which develop more complex and allegedly more realistic conceptions of belief? Let me stress that this work falls well outside the focus of therapeutic Bayesianism, for there is no reason to believe that such improvements will help to solve the standard problems in the philosophy of science. Perhaps these developments are important in psychology, statistics, semantics, or decision theory; perhaps they will become important to philosophy when we have progressed enough in our understanding of science so that the *details* of an inductive logic become items of reasonable concern. But at this juncture, confusion is rampant, the traditional problems are still very much with us, and it seems rather unlikely that the slight gains in accuracy to be derived from a more realistic theory of belief would be worth the price—in terms of loss of simplicity—that we would have to pay for it.

Our treatment of the 'raven paradox' is a case in point. The problem was solved by exposing a certain misconception (that a non-black, non-raven would be irrelevant to our hypothesis), and by explaining why we are so tempted by that misconception: namely, that in forgetting about degrees of belief, we lose sight of the distinction between very slight confirmation and no confirmation at all. The simple Bayesian model of belief provides a sufficiently perspicuous representation of the situation to enable us to put this in a clear way. Further accuracy regarding the nature of belief would distract us from the main point, ruin the argument, and not help us to understand the basis of the paradox.

Let me give another example. The conflict between realism and instrumentalism with respect to the acceptance of scientific theories is fuelled by a shared tendency to think in terms of all-or-nothing belief. The instrumentalist argues, in light of previous scientific revolutions, that it is foolishly optimistic to expect that our current theories are true and will not eventually be refuted. Whereas the realist complains that it is a distortion of science to distinguish rigidly between credible observation reports and incredible theoretical claims. However, once we see that the issue is not 'To believe or not to believe?' but rather, 'To what degree shall we believe?', then there is room for reconciliation. The crucial move is the elimination of the shared misconception. There is no reason to think that a fancy model of belief, even more accurate than the Bayesian idealization, would be any further help with the problem.

I do not mean to be suggesting that it is not worthwhile to investigate more sophisticated models of belief. On the contrary, I can readily imagine research programmes—e.g. Bayesian psychology, or attempts to give a perfectly accurate description of scientific practice—in which this would be crucial. My point is that there is another enterprise—the one I am calling 'therapeutic Bayesianism'—whose focus is on solving the traditional methodological puzzles and paradoxes, and for which the introduction of such complex models is likely to do more harm than good.

Suppose, then, that we do have numerical degrees of belief. Is there any way of justifying the Bayesian assumption that, to be rational, these degrees of belief must conform to the probability calculus? Although there are indeed various lines of reasoning which purport to establish this thesis, none is compelling. The best known of them is the 'dutch book' argument[8] and it goes roughly as follows. Defining a person's degree of belief in a proposition as

---

[8] For a good assessment of this argument and various others see John Earman's *Bayes or Bust* (Cambridge, Mass.: Harvard University Press, 1992). Bruno de Finetti perhaps deserves the credit for first having argued that degrees of belief *ought* to be 'coherent', i.e. conform to the probability calculus—though they *need* not be coherent if the believer is irrational: 'Foresight: Its Logical Laws, its Subjective Sources', tr. in H. E. Kyburg, Jr., and H. E. Smokler (eds.), *Studies in Subjective Probability* by (New York: John Wiley, 1964). I hesitate to credit Frank Ramsey's earlier paper, in D. H. Mellor (ed.), *Foundations: Essays in Philosophy, Logic, Mathematics and Economics* (Atlantic Highlands, NJ: Routledge & Kegan Paul, 1977), with this result, since he defines 'degrees of belief' in such a way that they *must* conform to the probability calculus. On Ramsey's account there is no room for the existence of someone who has degrees of belief that are not coherent.

a function of the odds at which he is prepared to bet on its truth, it can be proved that if his degrees of belief do not satisfy the probability calculus then he will be prepared to accept a collection of bets which is guaranteed to lead to a loss. Therefore, since it would surely be irrational for him knowingly to put himself in such a no-win situation, it would be irrational to have a system of degrees of belief that violates the probability calculus. QED. However, the definition of 'degree of belief' that is employed in this argument presupposes that people maximize their expected utility. And there is a lot of room for scepticism about that assumption (and about the preference axioms to which it is equivalent). So the 'dutch book' argument is far from airtight. Worse still, there is positive reason to think that its conclusion is false, for it requires logical omniscience. The probability of any logical truth is 1 and of any contradiction is 0. Yet it is surely quite rational to be less than perfectly confident in the truth of *some* logical truths—those that are especially hard to prove—and quite rational to give non-zero degrees of belief to contradictions that are hard to recognize as such.

The proper response to these difficulties is to repeat that the picture of rational degrees of belief obeying the probability calculus should be regarded as an *idealization* of the real normative facts. It is uncontroversial that one ought to be certain of elementary logical truths, and that one ought not to be confident of the truth of obviously incompatible hypotheses. The probabilistic model of belief provides a sharp, perspicuous way of capturing these trivialities, and to the extent that it goes beyond them it need not be construed realistically.

A similar answer may be given to the third question concerning the definition of confirmation. In our discussion of the raven paradox we defined 'the degree by which E confirms H' as 'the ratio, $P(H/E)/P(H)$, for a rational person'. Evidently, this explication has at least *some* prima-facie plausibility, and it certainly helps us to give a neat, compelling solution to the problem. Nonetheless, it is often argued that this particular explication is 'wrong'—yielding

counterintuitive consequences—and that there are better definitions of confirmation which should be used instead.[9]
However, these criticisms have little relevance to the project
of therapeutic Bayesianism. No doubt our explication leads to some
strange-sounding consequences. No doubt it is strictly speaking
false that the ordinary meaning of 'confirms' is given by our
explication. No doubt there are definitions (perhaps involving non-
probabilistic notions) that come even closer to what we ordinarily
mean. But the object of therapeutic Bayesianism is not to give a
theory of science. We are not trying to find the most accurate analyses of our concepts, but rather to use explications that are at least
roughly right, and which are conducive to simple, convincing disso-
lutions of philosophical problems. Since we assume that these problems are the product of confusion, it is desirable to look for ways of
clarifying the issues, which have the proper blend of accuracy and
simplicity. Of course it is possible to *over*simplify. But one can conclude that this has happened only after finding that the admittedly
idealized models do not in fact help to solve our problems.[10]

[9] For example, I. J. Good (in the *British Journal for the Philosophy of Science* 19
(1968), 123–43) advocates:

Weight of evidence concerning H provided by E $= \log \dfrac{P(E/H)}{P(E/-H)}$

And Seidenfeld (n. 7), noting that on our account E might confirm both H_1 and H_2
yet disconfirm the conjunction (H_1 and H_2), suggests that confirmation cannot be
defined in terms of probability alone.

[10] A further complaint is that our definition of confirmation seems to go badly
wrong when we apply it to measure the evidential value of *already known* data. For
in that case $P(E) = 1$, therefore $P(H/E) = P(H)$. This problem for Bayesians was first
posed by Clark Glymour (see his *Theory and Evidence* (Princeton: Princeton
University Press, 1980). It has been forcefully reiterated by James Woodward (in
his review of *P&E*, *Erkenntnis*, 23 (1985), 213–19) and is treated thoroughly by
John Earman (in *Bayes or Bust*). In order to deal with it we should remember that
the idea of the definition is to compare the credibility of a hypothesis, H, given the
knowledge that E is true, with its credibility in the absence of such knowledge. Thus
we should take the prior probability to be that which H would have had if the truth
of E had not been discovered. Then, in order to assess E's confirmation power, we

On the fourth question—are there objective facts of confirmation?—it seems evident that judgements of credibility and confirmation do purport to capture objective normative facts. They do not state what any individual's degrees of belief *actually* are, but rather they say something about what one's degrees of belief *ought* to be, or how they *ought* to change given the circumstances. Thus we should acknowledge non-subjective facts regarding confirmation.

A natural way of capturing this idea, due to Carnap, is to suppose that an attribution of probability to a hypothesis reflects the belief in an objective, logical fact about the degree to which one statement— a summary of the available evidence—probabilifies another statement—the hypothesis in question. Such logical facts might be codified in a confirmation function, $c(p/q) = x$, which would specify explicitly the degree, x, to which q confirms p, and would specify implicitly the degree to which one should believe p if the total evidence is q. Carnap says, for example:

> Probability-1 is the degree of confirmation of a hypothesis h with respect to an evidence statement e, e.g., an observation report. This is a logical, semantical concept. A sentence about this concept is based, not on observation of facts, but on logical analysis; if it is true, it is L-true (analytic). . . . Probability-2 [relative frequency] is obviously an objective concept. It is important to recognize that probability-1 is likewise objective.

> Let h be the sentence 'there will be rain tomorrow' and j the sentence 'there will be rain and wind tomorrow'. Suppose someone makes the statement in deductive logic: 'h follows logically from j'. . . . The statement 'the probability-1 of h on the evidence e is 1/5' has the same general character as the former statement. . . . Both statements express a purely logical relation between two statements. The difference

---

should consider what the absolute subjective probability of E would have been in that counterfactual situation, and also what the conditional probability of E given H would have been. Then we can employ Bayes's Theorem to calculate the factor by which the prior probability of H would have been increased. Doubtless, there is substantial indeterminacy in the assessment of these counterfactual probabilities. But this is no objection, since we generally have no reason to expect the magnitude of E's confirmation-power to be a perfectly determinate matter.

between the two statements is merely this: while the first states a complete logical implication, the second states, so to speak, a partial logical implication; hence, while the first belongs to deductive logic, the second belongs to inductive logic.[11]

Thus, Carnap held that certain facts about confirmation are analytic and *objective*, and thought of inductive probability as a *partial* version of the logical relation of entailment.[12]

On the fifth question—does reason impose constraints on belief *over and above* the requirement of conformity with the probability calculus?—there are grounds for sympathy with Carnap's view that it does. For it is hard to see how the probabilistic constraint alone can account for our intuitions about the relative plausibility of competing hypotheses that equally well fit the current data. In particular, it is hard to see how it can solve the 'grue' problem.[13]

Suppose that such further constraints are indeed required. Still, to take up the sixth question, it is no trivial matter to say what they are. Carnap tried out various constraints and employed them to derive confirmation functions for certain extremely simple formal languages. Unfortunately, these functions have the counterintuitive property that laws of nature are never able to acquire more than a negligible probability. And this shows a deficiency in Carnap's

---

[11] Rudolf Carnap, *Logical Foundations of Probability* (Chicago: University of Chicago Press, 1962), 19, 31.

[12] According to Spielman, this construal of Carnap is a 'distorted caricature' (170), for 'any careful reading of LFP [*Logical Foundations of Probability*] would show that Carnap never talks about "objective relations of probabilification" or "objective" relations of partial entailment' (170). Here I am at a loss to explain how Spielman could have arrived at his interpretation, and I can only refer the reader back to Carnap's work.

[13] Defining 'x is grue', à la Goodman, as 'x is green and examined before 1/1/3000 or x is blue and not examined before 1/1/3000', the problem is to explain why our data that all emeralds examined so far are green (and therefore grue) should confirm 'All emeralds are green' more strongly than it confirms 'All emeralds are grue', and should lead us to expect, as a consequence, that an emerald examined after 1/1/3000 will be green rather than blue. It is hard to see how this problem could be solved merely in terms of the requirement that our beliefs conform to the probability calculus. For further discussion of this point see *P&E* 32–6 and 74–81, and Earman's *Bayes or Bust*, ch 6.

constructions: either the languages are too simple, or the constraints are wrong. However, one can certainly not conclude that anyone who endorses a Carnapian conception of logical probability *must* hold that general laws never attain a non-negligible probability. This is a nonsequitur, arising from a failure to distinguish between the general conception of logical probability and the admittedly inadequate prototypes with which Carnap experimented.[14]

For the treatment of various problems it is helpful to suppose that inductive reasoning is represented by a specific (but unspecified) real-valued Carnapian confirmation function, c, allowing general laws to achieve a non-negligible credibility. In light of our responses to questions (1), (2), and (3), we see that it can be no objection to this procedure that our inductive practice is not in fact precisely described by a single c-function. For, once again, the intention is not to get at the exact truth, but merely to employ a useful idealization. Nor—as we have just said—is it fair to complain that *some* c-functions—those Carnap toyed with—always give zero probability to general laws. For we can suppose that 'the right c-function' is one of those that do *not* have that counterintuitive feature.

3. *Misplaced Scientism*

Much criticism of therapeutic Bayesianism arises from a conflation of philosophy and science. More exactly, it derives from a failure to recognize the legitimacy (even the existence) of non-scientific philosophical projects—those prompted, not by a desire to expose the whole truth regarding some domain, but by an interest in the resolution of paradoxes. Let me elaborate.

What one might call '*theory*-oriented philosophy of science' aims for a systematic account of the scientific method. The criteria

---

[14] Spielman (171) falls into this error, complaining that one cannot endorse logical probability and yet still assume that laws can have a non-negligible credibility.

of success are just those that pertain to theory construction *within* particular sciences: namely, empirical adequacy, scope, depth, simplicity, internal consistency, and coherence with the rest of our knowledge. More specifically, a perfect theory of the scientific method would be expected to conform with specific intuitions about the way that good science is done, to cover all aspects of methodology in detail, to expose fundamental principles enabling the complex, superficial aspects of scientific practice to be unified and explained, and to respect results in psychology and sociology. Thus it seems appropriate to regard theory-oriented philosophy of science as itself a department of science—a branch of naturalized epistemology. This characterization neither ignores nor denies that scientific methods are normative. A description of science will contain a codification of the basic norms which are implicit in the evaluation of theories. Moreover, it is quite possible that an identification of basic normative principles will result in the exposure of cases in which science is being done badly. One might thereby effect an improvement in the conduct of some science. Indeed, this may well be a motive for engaging in theory-oriented philosophy of science.

In contrast, the approach portrayed in this paper, 'problem-oriented philosophy of science', has very different goals, methods, and adequacy conditions. It aims at the resolution of deep puzzles and paradoxes that arise from reflection upon science. It includes in its domain, for example, the problem of induction, the paradox of confirmation, the question of total evidence, and the issue of prediction versus accommodation. The problems here are not simply to fill various undesirable gaps in our knowledge about science. Characteristically, they are conceptual tensions, contradictions, absurd conclusions—that is to say, symptoms of confusion. We have somehow gone astray, and the task is to understand how this has happened and to get a clear view of the issue so that our misguided ways of thinking will be exposed and no longer seem so attractive.

These two approaches to the philosophy of science do not compete with one another. They are distinct projects with distinct objectives—not *wholly* unrelated to one another, but by no means simply parts of the same enterprise. Thus, it is not the case that the sort of full understanding provided by a successful theory-oriented philosophy of science would automatically solve the puzzles that form the domain of problem-oriented philosophy of science. For the resolution of a paradox requires a great deal more than just locating the wrong move in a fallacious argument. It is crucial to a proper resolution that one comes to see why that fallacy was natural. And it is important that one obtains a new perspective on the issue—a point of view from which the old and troublesome habits of thought no longer seem plausible. These elements of the solution do not simply fall out of a complete theory of science. (Similarly, the explanations of conjuring tricks do not follow from physics.) Thus, theory-oriented philosophy of science is not simply a more thorough, systematic, and ambitious project than problem-oriented philosophy of science.

Nor is it necessary, in order to solve problems, that one be in possession of an adequate theory of science. For confusions can be identified, understood, and removed without a theory of any particular depth or generality. Granted, assumptions about methodology will often be involved in the diagnosis and treatment of a problem, and if these were *wildly* false then it is unlikely that the discussion would be helpful. However, there is no reason why such assumptions should be *true* as long as their replacement with the truth would not undermine the solution that is based on them. Indeed, it is quite possible that the perfect theory of science would be a very bad tool for solving problems. For the truth may be so complicated that it cannot provide the sort of simple and relevant perspective that is needed.

If the practice of conceptual troubleshooting is confused, as it often is, with the scientific search for a theory of science, then therapeutic Bayesianism will be wrongly subjected to all of the methodological requirements that are properly applied only in science. Let me describe some of the bad effects of this confusion.

One consequence, discussed above, of not seeing the distinctive aim of therapeutic Bayesianism is a tendency to misjudge the function of various helpful idealizations. Thus one commonly finds objections to the use of precise-valued degrees of belief, to the assumption that these should conform to the probability calculus, to the adoption of a particularly simple explication of confirmation, and to the idea that our inductive practice may be represented by a single Carnapian confirmation function. Doubtless some of these assumptions are, strictly speaking, false. (Just as it is false that a gas is made of point masses.) And in a different kind of study—one aimed at truth—it would be very important to discuss more realistic models. However, for the purposes of therapeutic Bayesianism, it is important to use the simplest roughly accurate models of degrees of belief and of confirmation that will help to clarify the issues, and it is sufficient to proceed on the basis of their intuitive plausibility and to justify these models in retrospect in terms of their utility.

Secondly, a scientific understanding of confirmation aims for the truth, the *whole* truth, and nothing but the truth. Consequently, those wedded to this conception of the philosophy of science will find fault with studies that do not discuss every significant aspect of the phenomenon of confirmation. Consider, for example, *prior probability assignment*, i.e. the procedures for deciding, before data have been gathered, the various 'intrinsic' plausibilities of hypotheses; *belief-kinematics*, the way that systems of belief change over time in the light of new discoveries; or *direct inference*, the impact on our degrees of belief of a knowledge of empirical probabilities. These are fascinating topics, and a good theory of science must deal with them. But there is no reason why a paradox-oriented Bayesian programme should incorporate a complete, systematic account of all such elements of methodology.[15]

In the third place, scientism in philosophy engenders a 'hyperformalist' fixation on symbolic technique—an overvaluation

---

[15] Thus Woodward writes: 'The principal defect of *Probability and Evidence* is its unsystematic character. Horwich does not give us a fully worked out general theory of confirmation but rather a series of essays which offer solutions to various particular puzzles, where the interconnections among these solutions are by no means always clear' (214).

of logico-mathematical machinery. Among the symptoms of this hyperformalist state are: (a) a blindness to the possibility of philosophical problems distinct from the scientific and mathematical issues that arise in statistics, decision theory, sociology of science, etc., further questions being dismissed as 'merely verbal';[16] (b) a dissatisfaction with informal discussions and conclusions; (c) an exaggerated concern with formal rigour for its own sake; and (d) an obsession with the elimination of any potential ambiguity or vagueness, leading to the feeling that the English language is too confusing and vague a medium for intellectual progress, and that it should, wherever possible, be replaced with mathematics or logic.

Thus, even if an approach employs formal techniques, as therapeutic Bayesianism clearly does, it may still be subjected to hyperformalist criticism. I think this is an unhealthy point of view—in philosophy generally, and particularly in the philosophy of science, where it is especially common. No doubt there are occasions when clarity is gained and confusion allayed with the help of formal apparatus. This, I believe, is one of the morals of Bayesianism's success. However, one can withdraw too quickly into the secure, regulated territory of a formal system. It is certainly a tempting relief from the frustrating vagaries of philosophy to be able to obtain definite, proven results and get clear answers to clear questions. But, unless we are very careful, these answers and results might have little to do with the problems that have traditionally motivated philosophy of science. Our methodological puzzles arise

---

[16] This is starkly revealed in Seidenfeld's dismissal of therapeutic Bayesianism on the grounds that it is no substitute for a combination of excellent, but highly technical, foundational studies in decision theory and statistical inference by Jeffrey, Fishburn, and Lindley—works that hardly touch upon the traditional philosophical puzzles that form the domain of therapeutic Bayesianism. In a similar vein, Spielman is bothered by the 'fail(ure) to see that the only difference between an "objectivist" account [of the "grue" problem] and a personalist account would be verbal: an objectivist would say that we *ought* to assign a much higher probability to H_1 than to H_2, and a subjectivist says that this is what intelligent informed people in fact do' (170). Spielman thinks the issue between them is 'merely verbal'.

when we reflect informally about scientific practice; and they can be solved only with an appreciation of the misconceptions and confusions to which we are prone and an understanding of the ways in which they are fostered by the rich conceptual resources put at our disposal by natural language. It seems to me that only when that sort of understanding is eventually attained will we know what we are looking for in a fully fledged inductive logic; and then, perhaps, be in a better position to devise one. But this level of understanding will not be achieved by trying to express as many questions as possible within a formal system, proving some theorems, and dismissing the residue as intractable and uninteresting. At its worst, such scientistic hyperformalism betrays a lack of concern for truly philosophical problems. If 'merely verbal' issues are any that do not make a scientific difference, and if only scientific problems are worth worrying about, then philosophy is truly an endangered enterprise.

I hope to have clarified what I believe is a valuable approach to the philosophy of science, and to have shown that many of the complaints about it derive from scientistic hyperformalism and are therefore misconceived. The goal is not a theory of science but the unravelling of puzzles surrounding our ideas about surprising data, prediction versus accommodation, *ad hoc* postulates, statistical hypotheses, our thirst for new data, the tenability of realism, and other aspects of methodology. And given some of the successes of therapeutic Bayesianism, there is reason to have a fair amount of confidence in its basic principles.

Thus, the notion of rational degrees of belief conforming to the probability calculus has an important role in the philosophy of science. It would no doubt be easier to think in terms of all-or-nothing belief, but that oversimplification is part of what engendered our methodological puzzles in the first place. On the other hand, there are more complex and realistic conceptions of belief, but the cause of clarity is not served by using them. Therapeutic Bayesianism appears to offer the ideal compromise between accuracy and simplicity, enabling us to represent the issues starkly without neglecting the essential ingredients or clouding them with unnecessary details.

7 Deflating the Direction of Time

The traditional aim of metaphysics is to uncover, by a priori means, those fundamental ingredients of reality that lie beneath the reach of empirical inquiry. But these days such projects are well out of philosophical fashion. After the devastating attacks on a priori theorizing by Wittgenstein and by Quine, it is now widely believed that the sciences exhaust what can be known, and that the promise of metaphysics is an intellectually dangerous illusion. An anti-metaphysical naturalism dominates philosophical research. J. R. Lucas stands in opposition to this current mainstream of thought, insisting on a distinction between 'the aspects of reality that scientific investigation can discover' and 'the full nature of reality itself'. However, his book on the metaphysics of time, so full of ingenuity, subtlety, and intelligence, illustrates just how difficult it is to sustain that premise.[A]

The primary point of the book is to oppose a certain simple and scientifically adequate picture: namely, that time is a linear array of instants at which physical and mental events are located, an infinite continuum stretching from the past through the present and into the future. Leaving aside the complications introduced by relativity theory, which are irrelevant here, this picture is championed by most philosophers of time—for example, Russell, Reichenbach, Grunbaum, Smart, and Earman—and is more or less taken for granted in science itself. But according to Lucas it:

> gives a deeply inadequate view of time. It fails to account for the passage of time, the pre-eminence of the present, the directedness of time

[A] The book under discussion is Lucas's *The Future* (Oxford: Blackwell, 1987).

and the difference between future and past, and has to make out that these fundamental aspects of our experience and thought are merely psychological and linguistic aberrations. It also fails to accommodate the concept of agency, the belief that we can make up our minds for ourselves, and that it is up to us what we decide and what we do. And it runs counter to the thrust of quantum mechanics, the most fundamental physical theory that we have, which portrays a universe that is not determinist but only probabilistic.

One might very well wonder whether there is really any incompatibility between the scientific picture of time and the various phenomena that Lucas mentions. For the feeling of time passing might be explained, it would seem, without supposing that time itself is 'flowing'. The pre-eminence of the present could be attributed to the complex structure of an experience, to its division into anticipation, sensation, and memory. And, as for the *directedness* of time, whether such a thing exists, and needs to be accounted for, is presumably just what is at issue. Moreover, the fact that these matters may be dealt with in terms of the linear model does not make them 'aberrations'. It is, rather, the ways Lucas favours of characterizing them that become aberrations. Moving on to the other alleged problems, the conflict he claims to find between freedom and linear time is familiar from Aristotle. But, as we shall see, Lucas's own analysis suffices to undermine the Aristotelian position, so it is somewhat surprising that he should endorse it. Finally, there is no contradiction between the suppositions (*a*) that what will happen is not causally determined by prior events and (*b*) that one can now make true predictions (perhaps by chance) about what will happen. We can, therefore, accept both the linear model of time and indeterministic theories such as quantum mechanics. Thus it is by no means clear that the linear model runs into difficulties of the kind that Lucas mentions.[B]

[B] For further discussion of how to explain away these apparent indicators of temporal passage and anisotropy, see my *Asymmetries in Time* (Cambridge, Mass.: MIT Press, 1987), chs. 1 and 2.

However, he does not address such doubts, apparently taking it for granted that his concerns are at least *prima facie* plausible, and he proceeds with the attempt to construct what he takes to be a better model—one in which:

> Time is the passage from possibility through actuality to unalterable necessity . . . Whereas the present, and past are real, the future, as long as it is still future, is not; only by becoming present is it actualized into reality: hence the passage and the direction of time.

Thus, according to Lucas, reality resembles an unlimited tree: from any point there is a single definite path downward (history is fixed) but above each point we encounter a proliferation of many possible branches (the future is open). Therefore statements about the past are, right now, determinately true or false, unlike current claims about the future, which do not become true or false until the predicted events either occur or fail to occur. Only the advance of the NOW—a peculiar, 'pre-eminent', metaphysical index—settles which path through the tree is taken and which predictions are correct. This is indeed a natural and satisfying picture of time. However, the big question hanging over it is whether it can be converted from a suggestive image into a coherent theory—one that is even so much as *distinct* from, let alone superior to, our simple, scientific model. And this is more difficult than Lucas appears to recognize. Let me explain.

The central question of the book is whether the future exists; that is, whether a proposition can *now* be true if what it states is that some contingent event will take place *later*. To borrow Aristotle's example, can it be true today that there will be a sea-battle tomorrow? According to the scientific model the answer is yes. Just as there is some particular course of events that makes up our history, so there is a particular collection of events (about which we can, admittedly, know very little) that occupies the future; and a prediction is now true just in case the predicted event is a member of that collection. Now Lucas *says* that he rejects this picture and *claims* to be articulating an alternative in which, though the past and present are definite and real, the future contains nothing but a manifold of branching possibilities. In that spirit, we find him maintaining that propositions about future times typically do not become true until those times become present.

However, it emerges on closer scrutiny that these theses do not mean what they superficially seem to mean, and do not really conflict with the scientific model. The impression to the contrary comes from the fact that Lucas employs the expression 'proposition about the future' in his own special way. He puts unusual weight on the difference between the *simple future* tensed statement, 'There *will be* a sea-battle tomorrow', and the *posterior present* tensed statement. 'There *is going to be* a sea-battle tomorrow', which he idiosyncratically takes to mean 'Present circumstances *guarantee* that there will be a sea-battle tomorrow'. The former will turn out to have been true if a sea-battle happens to occur, even if it occurs by sheer chance; the latter is true only if events at the time it was asserted *ensure*, via laws of nature, that a sea-battle will certainly take place. But since, quite plausibly, it is *not* now causally determined what will happen tomorrow, it follows that one must reject the disjunction, 'Either there is going to be a sea-battle tomorrow or there is going to be no sea-battle tomorrow'. So it may appear that Lucas is, in some sense, denying the reality of the future. But in fact he is doing no such thing. He has no quarrel with a parallel claim in the simple future tense: namely, 'There will be a sea-battle tomorrow or there will be no sea-battle tomorrow', which implies that some definite statement about the future would now be true. Thus what he is denying is merely that the future is *determined by present conditions*, and not that it exists. Once his somewhat specialized way of putting things is rephrased in ordinary English it turns out that Lucas's position is not the controversial metaphysical doctrine that it was advertised to be: that many alternatives are *possible* is quite consistent with the naive and scientific view that one of them will *actually* transpire.

Another place at which there is less of substance than one might
at first suppose is Lucas's discussion of the *passage* of time. Here
again he finds the anti-metaphysical view inadequate—that each
utterance of the word 'now' refers to whatever the time is at which
it occurs (just as 'here' refers to whatever is the place at which it is
uttered). He believes that the 'motion of NOW' is a profound,
objective feature of the world which is not captured by the conception of time as a linear array. But it is far from clear what is supposed to be missing from this simple, scientific model. It is a trivial
fact that, at any time, *that* particular time is appropriately called
'now'; or, as one might put it, that the location of NOW at any time
is *that* time. It is clear, moreover, that *the* direction of a change
between various states is, by definition, the direction *from* whatever are the earlier *to* whatever are the later of these states—and
therefore *the* direction of change in the location of NOW is from
earlier to later locations of NOW. It is easy to see therefore that the
direction of change in the location of NOW is from earlier to later
times; and in the same vein, that all future events will eventually
become present and then recede into the past. None of this is in any
way controversial or mysterious; none of it goes beyond what
McTaggart called 'B-series facts'; and contrary to Lucas's initial
complaint it shows that the scientific model can easily accommodate the direction of time. However, Lucas aligns himself with those
philosophers (such as Bergson and McCall)—the advocates of
'absolute becoming', 'temporal passage', and 'the moving NOW'
—who contend that time involves something deeper than what has
just been described and what is universally acknowledged. Time,
they say, *really* passes; the motion of NOW is *genuine*, not just an
artefact of language. The trouble is that nobody has ever been able
to articulate, clearly and consistently, what this doctrine comes to.

Consider again Lucas's account of time flow, quoted above, as the
transition from possibility via actuality to necessity. If the universe
is indeterministic with respect to the future and not with respect to
the past, then at any time t there will be a single possible course

of events stretching back into the past and a manifold of branching possibilities stretching into the future. Thus, at time *t* the location of the *initial branch point* is at time *t*. Now we have already seen how it is perfectly legitimate, indeed trivial, to hold that *the present* changes its temporal location in the direction from past to future. We have seen that this 'directionality of time' stems from the time-bias that is built into our definition of '*the* direction of a change' (i.e. as the direction from earlier to later states). For exactly the same reasons we can see that (in a world that is indeterministic just toward the future) the location of the initial branch point moves in the direction from past to future. In neither case does the particular direction of time flow result from any asymmetry in the structure of time itself. In both cases it derives from the time-asymmetry in our rules for the use of the expression '*the* direction of a change'. It seems to me therefore that, although Lucas may sympathize with the proponents of a *genuinely* moving now, his actual theory of time flow belongs in the opposition camp. The sort of time flow represented in his model is not at all controversial.

Each of the points I have discussed illustrates a classic difficulty in metaphysical theorizing: managing to steer a course between uncontroversial triviality on the one hand and incomprehensible nonsense on the other. In the face of this problem one response is to employ technical jargon and idiosyncratic uses of familiar terms in such a way that the truistic character of the 'theory' is disguised (even from its proponents). Another common strategy is to say something that, taken literally, is perfectly obvious and universally accepted, but then to indicate by means of various devices (such as emphatic table thumping and the careful insertion of words like 'really' and 'genuinely') that something different from normal, and much more profound, is intended. Thus we hear 'Numbers *really* exist', 'That lying is wrong is a *genuine* fact', and so on. Of course such responses to the difficulty are not satisfactory, and unless better ones can be found we will be left with the quite reasonable suspicion that in fact no metaphysical theory is called for and that the apparent need for one is based on confusion.[C] Lucas appears to be a victim of this predicament. Although he bills himself as an advocate of 'time flow' and of 'the unreality of the future', his *explanations* of these ideas shows that what he has in mind is something that the anti-metaphysical naturalists can happily accept.

[C] These meta-philosophical points are amplified in Essay 10.

8   Gibbard's Theory of Norms

That we should care about rationality goes without saying. For to
be rational is to be as one *should* be, and presumably, whatever way
of being that is is a way that we should wish to be. Therefore, we
rightly want to know what the norms of rationality are, such
knowledge being necessary, or at least helpful, if we are to obey and
enforce them. However, we can hardly ever agree on exactly what
they are, or even on how to find out. And in such situations philosophers naturally turn to matters of clarification and ask what it
means to call something 'rational', 'right', or 'the wise choice'.

Contemporary opinion on this sort of metanormative question is
divided into two camps, and much of the current discussion consists
of arguments between them. On one side there are the self-styled
realists (also known as descriptivists and cognitivists), who hold
that normative assertions aim to describe a portion of reality—a
realm of normative properties and normative facts, which we are
somehow able to discern and which make our claims about what is
rational either true or false. On the other side there are the emotivist, noncognitivist anti-realists, who hold that evaluative utterances are merely expressions of feeling, neither true nor false, not
even purporting to correspond to facts—so that sceptical questions

A review of Allan Gibbard, *Wise Choices, Apt Feelings: A Theory of Normative
Judgment* (Oxford: Oxford University Press, 1990). I am indebted to Joshua Cohen
and Robert Stalnaker for the many things I learnt from our numerous discussions of
rationality in general and Gibbard's book in particular. I would like to thank them,
together with Ned Block, Peter Railton, Georges Rey, and the editors of *Philosophy
and Public Affairs*, for helpful comments on an earlier draft of this essay.

cannot arise with respect to them. In *Wise Choices, Apt Feelings: A Theory of Normative Judgment* Allan Gibbard enters the fray on the side of the emotivists, and the great value of his book lies in the unprecedented depth, rigour, and plausibility that he brings to the point of view. He argues, to my mind convincingly, that rationality is not a naturalistic property, neither simple nor complex. But this potentially puzzling conclusion is allowed to leave no sense of mystery; for the overall tenor of the book—in particular, the examination of our *thought* about rationality—is highly naturalistic. Both the psychological role and the biological origins of such thought are explained in detail. And this treatment is extended into ethics by virtue of an ingenious analysis of moral concepts in terms of the conditions for rational feelings of guilt and shame.

As Gibbard observes at the outset, 'rational' is an ambiguous term, and it is with just one of its senses that he is going to be concerned. This is the sense in which it may be predicated of a wide variety of cognitive entities (including beliefs, actions, desires, and feelings), in which it appears to express a positive evaluation (some sort of endorsement or recommendation), and in which we might well substitute terms such as 'sensible', 'justified', or 'best', or use some construction involving 'ought' or 'should'. When we say, 'One ought not be *too* rational; a bit of spontaneity is a good thing', we are using the word 'rational' in a different way (meaning 'calculating', or something of the sort). Or we may intend something like 'conducive to narrow self-interest' and ask, in this sense, whether it is 'rational' to care about the welfare of others. But this again is not the general, endorsing concept of rationality that Gibbard has in mind.

Supposing that there is such a concept, Gibbard separates various types of questions that may be raised with respect to it:

1. Substantive: What is rational?
2. Metaphysical: What sort of entity, if any, is rationality?
3. Semantic: What does the word 'rational' mean?
4. Epistemological: How do we find out what is rational?

5. Functional: What utility has the concept of rationality?
6. Biological: Why do we have the concept of rationality?

The semantic question 'What does the word "rational" mean?' must be distinguished, Gibbard emphasizes, from the substantive question 'What is rational?' (or, 'Under what circumstances is an action or belief rational?'). It is one thing, he says, to devise a theory that tells us systematically which things are rational and which are not; it is quite another thing to provide a *definition* of 'rational': that is, an account of what those who advocate different theories are disagreeing about. Moreover, the substantive question must be distinguished from the epistemological question 'How do we find out what is rational?' True, we may rely on a substantive theory to determine, in individual cases, whether something is rational or not. We may, for example, use the theory of expected utility maximization to find out what should be done. However, it remains to be shown how we arrive at this theory in the first place.

Looming over the entire cluster of questions is a metaquestion, namely, 'Why ask?' Why is rationality of philosophical concern? Part of the answer, as I have said, is that it is both important and difficult to determine what rationality requires, and so we switch our attention to the meta-issues in the hope of gaining clarification and insight. In addition, however, rationality is a peculiarly intriguing concept because, in *its* case, one is hard pressed to see how a satisfactory combination of answers is possible. In particular, it is notoriously difficult to think of responses to the semantic question that could square with a satisfactory answer to the functional one. To put the problem less abstractly: (*a*) There appear to be facts about what it is rational to do, to want, to feel, and to think. (*b*) We are far from impervious to such facts. That is, our recognition of them has motivational force; to some degree we want to be rational and want those we care about to be rational too. However, (*c*) we cannot find any account of the underlying nature of the normative facts that would explain this motivational force. We do not see what it is about the

character of rationality that makes it conceptually anomalous—
perhaps even incoherent—to think that someone might regard a
norm as rational and yet have no inclination to conform to it.

This problem is what makes rationality a mysterious notion. But
it is also the basis for the sort of account that Gibbard favours—
what he calls 'norm-expressivism'. His line of thought goes as
follows. First, we notice (paralleling G. E. Moore's so-called open-
question argument concerning the concept 'good')[1] that whatever
naturalistic definition F were proposed of the word 'rational', one
could coherently raise the question: 'Yes, I agree that so-and-so has
characteristic F; but is it rational?' Such reasoning might lead one
to suppose (as it did Moore in the case of 'good') that 'rational' is
an indefinable primitive. But this result would be unsatisfying,
because it would leave it inexplicable why we must be moved by
our beliefs about what is rational. The way out, says Gibbard (and
here he is influenced by the meta-ethical writings of A. J. Ayer,[2]
C. Stevenson,[3] and R. M. Hare[4]), is to recognize that there are ways
to specify the meaning of a word other than by giving a standard,
explicit definition of it (in the style of 'bachelor' means 'unmarried
man'); other, more complex forms of rules for its use will do. In the
present case we might offer an explicit definition of 'Y believes that
x is rational' and aim thereby to implicitly capture the meaning of
'rational'. The crude picture is that, given the meaning of 'Y
believes that x is rational', we can 'subtract' the known meaning of
'Y believes that . . . ' and thus obtain the meaning of 'rational'.
Moreover, by properly defining 'Y believes that x is rational' we
may hope to solve the above-mentioned problem that seemed insuperable for an explicit analysis of 'rational', that is, to account for
the fact that if someone believes that a certain norm is rational, he

---

[1] G. E. Moore, *Principia Ethica* (Cambridge: Cambridge University Press, 1903).

[2] A. J. Ayer, *Language, Truth and Logic* (2nd edn. London: Victor Gollancz, 1946).

[3] C. Stevenson, 'The Emotive Theory of Ethical Terms', *Mind*, 46 (1937), 14–31.

[4] R. M. Hare, *The Language of Morals* (Oxford: Oxford University Press, 1952).

must have some inclination to conform to it and some desire that his friends conform to it. For suppose the analysis of 'Y believes that norm x is rational' were something (very roughly) of the form 'Y has a pro-attitude toward being governed by x, and has a pro-attitude toward those he cares about being governed by x, and . . .' In that case it would follow immediately that views about what is rational have motivational force.[A]

Given some such analysis, and assuming also that assertions of p standardly express a belief *that p*, it can be inferred that assertions of the form 'x is rational' standardly express certain pro-attitudes. However, following the usual practice in meta-ethical discussions, Gibbard goes beyond this result and characterizes the expressivist view as one according to which when we call something rational we are *merely* expressing an attitude and *not* ascribing to it some property of *rationality*. So there will be no facts consisting of certain things being rational and others not, and attributions of rationality will be neither true nor false. It should be noted that these answers to the metaphysical questions of rationality are not deduced solely from the semantic thesis of norm-expressivism: a certain 'thick' conception of 'fact' is needed as well. Gibbard's line (following Gilbert Harman[5]) is to characterize facts (perhaps better called 'natural facts') as entities that have a role in the explanation of our beliefs about them. Therefore, facts of rationality do not exist, he argues, because the explanations of our beliefs about what is rational make

---

[A] A more general characterization of the 'expressivist' view of our concept of *ought* is that, in order for the word 'ought' to mean what it does, it must have the following property: namely, that its fundamental (i.e. underived) rule (or law) of use dictate a correlation between certain applications of the term (or of its mentalese associate) within someone's belief-box and appearances in his desire-box of what the term is applied to. The precise character of this correlation (including the range of different kinds of sentence containing 'ought' that must exhibit it) will vary from one expressivist account to another—the correct account being the one whose proposed basic rule for 'ought' gives the best explanation of its *overall* use. For further discussion of the view of meaning deployed here, see Essay 4.

[5] Gilbert Harman, *The Nature of Morality* (New York: Oxford University Press, 1977).

reference merely to the evolutionary benefits of the coordination fostered by our having such beliefs; it is never because a thing *is* rational that we think it is. Hence there are no facts or truths about what is rational, and there is no property of rationality.

Gibbard takes the main burden of his defence of norm-expressivism to be to reconcile its semantic, epistemological, and metaphysical theses with the familiar phenomena of normative discourse. For although norm-expressivism portrays normative notions as deeply different from naturalistic ones, nevertheless the appearance of normative discourse is strikingly similar to that of naturalistic discourse. In particular: (1) The predicate 'rational' occurs not merely in assertions of the form '*x* is rational' (to which norm-expressivism is explicitly addressed), but also embedded within logically complex constructions and standard patterns of argument, just as if it stood for a property: for example, 'She is highly rational; therefore, if that investment had been rational she would have made it; but she did not make it; so it must not have been rational.' (2) It is possible for one person to tell someone else what is rational. Some *content*—like a piece of information—appears to be communicated, and in that case the hearer may come to believe something of which he was previously unaware. (3) Normative claims purport to be objective. They are supposed to hold regardless of anyone's opinion, and they are asserted with an air of authority—with an expectation that they will be accepted by others.

That these phenomena are consistent with norm-expressivism is something Gibbard expends considerable space and ingenuity in attempting to establish. He thereby seeks to rebut the influential objection made by Peter Geach[6] (who attributes the basic insight to Frege) that such phenomena preclude an expressivist position. But it seems to me that not enough attention is given to motivating this concern in the first place; for, despite its pedigree, the existence of any real problem here is by no means obvious. The paradox is supposedly

---

[6] Peter Geach, 'Assertion', *Philosophical Review*, 74 (1964), 449–65.

that, on the one hand, normative claims are actually addressed and debated as though they were about facts; but, on the other hand, they are not (according to norm-expressivism) really factual. But this formulates a problem for norm-expressivism only if the term 'fact' is used in the same sense in both of its occurrences; and one might well wonder whether this is so. For Gibbard's official notion of 'fact', whereby rationality claims do not concern facts, is a notion of *natural fact*—for which certain explanatory characteristics have been stipulated, as we have seen. However, there is another, weaker, notion of fact—arguably the one to be found in ordinary language—whereby '*p*' and 'It is a fact that *p*' say more or less the same thing whatever meaningful declarative sentence is substituted for *p*. And, one might suspect that it is in this more liberal sense that normative claims are taken to be fact-stating in just the way that naturalistic claims are.

Let me expand this point a bit. There is a plausible *deflationary* account of truth (developed by Frank Ramsey,[7] A. J. Ayer,[8] P. Strawson,[9] and W. V. Quine[10]) according to which the function of the truth-predicate is not to *describe* propositions, as one might naively infer from its syntactic form, but rather to enable a certain type of generalization to be constructed. Consider, for example,

What Einstein said is true.

This may be used to express agreement with a proposition that one cannot identify explicitly. (Perhaps he was mumbling.) It is intuitively equivalent to the claim

If Einstein said that nothing goes faster than light, then nothing goes faster than light; and if Einstein said that religious belief is irrational, then religious belief is irrational; and . . .

[7] Frank Ramsey, 'Facts and Propositions', *Proceedings of the Aristotelian Society* (suppl.), 7 (1927), 153–70.

[8] Ayer, *Language, Truth and Logic*.

[9] P. Strawson, 'Truth', *Proceedings of the Aristotelian Society* (suppl.), 24 (1950), 129–56.

[10] W. V. Quine, *Pursuit of Truth* (Cambridge, Mass.: Harvard University Press, 1990).

We are able to capture this infinite conjunction with the help of the equivalence schema

The proposition *that p* is true if and only if *p*.

For on the basis of these biconditionals the initial conjunction may be reformulated as

If Einstein said that nothing goes faster than light, then the proposition *that nothing goes faster than light* is true; and if Einstein said that religious belief is irrational, then the proposition *that religious belief is irrational* is true; and . . .

And this can be summarized using the ordinary universal quantifier *every*, which generalizes over objects: that is,

For every *x*, if what Einstein said is *x*, then *x* is true.

Or, in other words,

What Einstein said is true.

It is arguable that all legitimate uses of the truth-predicate—including those in science, logic, semantics, and metaphysics—are simply displays of this generalizing function.[11] If this is right, we may conclude, first of all, that traditional theories, which identify truth with a substantive property (such as correspondence with reality, coherence, pragmatic utility, or provability), are mistaken. The trivial equivalence schema

The proposition *that p* is true if and only if *p*

is necessary and sufficient for the truth-predicate to perform its function, and so it provides an adequate theory, unsupplemented by any further account of 'what truth is'. Therefore, we have simply no reason to assume that truth has an 'underlying nature' remaining to be characterized. Second, every type of proposition—every

---

[11] I have attempted to make this case and explore its ramifications in *Truth* (Oxford: Basil Blackwell, 1990); 2nd edition, Oxford University Press, 1998.

possible object of belief, assertion, conjecture, and so on—will be a candidate for truth, for the device of generalization is no less useful when the propositions in question are normative than when they are naturalistic. And third, parallel accounts will hold of notions such as 'fact' and 'property' that are intimately related to 'truth'. Thus, according to the deflationary point of view, adequate theories of these notions are given, respectively, by the schemata

> *That p* is a fact if and only if *p*

and

> For any object *x*, *x* has the property of *being F* if and only if *x* is F.

(Though, as mentioned above, stronger notions of fact and property, satisfying naturalistic, explanatory requirements, may be constructed in addition.)

These ideas bear on Gibbard's theory in two respects. First, in so far as such deflationary accounts of truth, fact, and property capture our actual notions, it is wrong to say that normative claims do not concern facts, are not true, and do not attribute properties. Norm-expressivism has no need for these theses and would be better off without them. Its real substance lies in a distinctive semantic view of the indirect way in which the term 'rational' is defined (namely, that the meaning of 'rational' is specified implicitly by means of an explicit definition of 'Y believes that *x* is rational'), and a distinctive metaphysical claim about the nonexplanatory nature of normative facts (namely, that beliefs about what is rational are not consequences of what is in fact rational).

It might be objected that the renunciation of truth, facts, and properties in connection with normative concepts is such an entrenched and central aspect of the expressivist point of view that the change I am proposing would amount more to a rejection of the doctrine than to a mere revision of it. Arguably this is so; arguably the import of the deflationary theory of truth for metanormative discussion is best conceived of as an undermining of the received conflict between realists and expressivists, exposing a false, shared presupposition, and suggesting a third, 'mixed' alternative. It seems to me, however, that the semantic claim of expressivism, with its epistemological and functional consequences, retains its distinctive character and importance without the traditional further theses about truth, properties, and facts. And in an area already afflicted with an excess of 'isms' it seems preferable not to compose yet another one. Thus the moral of deflationism is that expressivism should be reformulated, not denied.

Second, in light of the senses in which normative claims do ascribe properties, are fact-stating, and do have truth-values, the extent to which normative and naturalistic discourse resemble one another and are mutually integrated is quite unsurprising. Indeed, it is precisely because the word 'rational' is given the same inferential role as most other predicates that it may be said to express a property and to help formulate facts and truths. Thus, given our predicative use of the term, it is trivial that 'rational' is significant even within complex constructions, that views about what is rational may be entertained and communicated, and that normative claims are presented as intersubjectively valid. The only possible question is whether such a use conflicts with the basic doctrines of norm-expressivism. But there is not the slightest reason to suspect any tension between implicitly constraining the meaning of 'rational' in the way described above and the further decision to treat the word as a normal predicate. Nor is there any reason to suspect that the explanatory peculiarity of rationality—that in virtue of which it is not a *natural* property—could jeopardize the predicate-like conceptual role of the term that expresses it. Thus there appears to be no prima-facie problem of understanding how normative and naturalistic discourse could be similar to one another.

The central point, once again, is that the expressivist is not obliged to explain, on the basis of his story about what is expressed by '*x* is rational', why 'rational' must have the inferential role of a predicate. All he needs to do is defend the prima-facie plausible assumption that to his story about '*x* is rational' he may consistently add the supposition that 'rational' has that role. And in the

absence of any reason whatsoever to suggest the contrary, the consistency of this conjunction of semantic principles hardly stands in need of defence. Just as 'x is white' is the standard expression of a belief that stems from a certain experience, so 'x is rational' is the standard expression of a belief that stems from certain pro-attitudes. In both cases we can suppose, in addition, that the terms are logical predicates, in both cases that their application is constrained by the speaker's states of mind, and in both cases that, given the basic physiological similarity between human beings, a fair measure of intersubjective agreement is to be expected.

As for the so-called Frege–Geach embedding problem, one is left wondering why it should be thought problematic at all. Allegedly, if 'x is rational' is said to be the expression of an attitude, then complex constructions such as If 'x is rational, . . . ' and 'Either x is rational or . . .' are deprived of sense. But once we have supplemented the expressivist analysis with the principle that 'rational' is a logical predicate, there is no reason to suspect that there are constructions involving that term whose deployment cannot be explained. And in that case, there is no reason to deny that norm-expressivism captures our concept. In other words, if our entire use of the term 'rational' can be explained on the assumption that the rules of use we have in mind are simply (1) 'Y believes that x is rational' means 'Y has a pro-attitude toward x and . . . ' and (2) 'rational' is a logical predicate, then we may conclude that it is in following these rules that our knowledge of the meaning of 'rational' consists.[B]

[B] It is commonly supposed (e.g. in Simon Blackburn's *Ruling Passions* (Oxford: Oxford University Press, 1998)) that an expressivist response to the Frege–Geach objection must involve some specification, for each logically complex construction containing 'ought', of which non-cognitive attitude is expressed by deploying that construction. This strategy has proved hard to carry out; but I think it was a mistake to have assumed that a decent response to the objection would have to take that form. For it is perfectly possible that the best basic rule for 'ought'—the one that best explains our overall use of it—correlates only certain *atomic* ought-claims with conative states. In that case, the mental states expressed by the logically complex pronouncements will be nothing more than beliefs.

So far I have discussed the *kind* of analysis of rationality that Gibbard is suggesting. Let me now turn to the particular one he proposes: namely, that, to a first approximation,

Y believes that x is rational

means

Y accepts norms that permit x.

Although Gibbard frequently highlights this view as 'the norm-expressivist analysis', its true role in his theory is left far from clear, for one might well feel that the analysans is just as problematic as the analysandum (as if he were defining 'rational' as justi-fied'). What, after all, does the analysans itself mean if not something like

Y believes that certain general principles about what is rational are correct, and those statements are consistent with the thesis that x is rational.

But this is not progress. The problem was to give some account of what 'rational' means that could explain the motivational force of beliefs about rationality, and this has not yet been done. Of course, one is at liberty to *supplement* the analysis, as Gibbard does, with a further theory according to which anyone in the state of 'accepting norms' will have some tendency to avow them and be governed by them, and one can hope to deal with the problem in this way. But still the overall view retains a couple of questionable features. First, the purpose of the analysis remains obscure. Why not simply apply the further theory directly to the state of 'believing that x is rational' and dispense altogether with the intermediate step? Why not, in other words, propose

Y is disposed to avow and be governed by norm x

as an account of what it is for Y to believe that x is a rational norm, and forget about acceptance? And second, why suggest, misleadingly I think, that the heart of norm-expressivism is the initial analysis? For it is only in the supplementary theory—the account of what is involved in accepting a norm—that a distinctively emotivist position emerges.

Another small anomaly concerns the *name* that Gibbard gives to his theory: 'norm-expressivism'. This term might seem apt because, according to the theory, the sentence '*x* is rational' is used to *express* a certain attitude toward certain *norms*. But the trouble is that *this* aspect of the theory is utterly uncontroversial. Wouldn't everybody agree—even those realists who hold that rationality is a natural property—that if one says '*x* is rational' then one is expressing some attitude (belief, perhaps) toward some norm? *Any* categorical utterance expresses some mental state, so the characterization of Gibbard's view as a form of 'expressivism' conveys no information about it.

Not that the other names in the literature are so much better. 'Noncognitivism' is often used to designate views like Gibbard's. However, such views should not, strictly speaking, *deny* that one can *believe* something to be rational; for what they really provide is an account of what any such belief consists in (that is, the possession of a certain pro-attitude). So the noncognitivist label is inappropriate. 'Anti-realism' is even worse, for it suggests the very metaphysical move—rejecting the *property* of rationality—that I have just criticized. The original term, 'emotivism', though imperfect, strikes me as the best, for at least it conveys the idea that claims of rationality are expressions of what might loosely be called 'feeling'.

Finally, a brief remark about the substantive question 'What is rational?' Answers to this question purport to specify systematically which actions, beliefs, desires, and feelings the word 'rational' applies to. For example, the theory that one should maximize expected utility purports to be a partial answer. Another answer is the theory that a belief is rational just in case it is one of a consistent system of beliefs. But the tendency of the considerable literature on decision theory and on inductive logic is to show that neither of these is satisfactory, even within their special domains; nor do there appear to be better alternatives waiting in the wings. Now although Gibbard's purpose in his book is not to provide substantive normative theories, he does suggest that his analysis will put us in a good position to find them. Indeed, he cites this as its chief virtue. But it strikes me, on the contrary, that norm-expressivism gives grounds for a certain scepticism with respect to the substantive question of rationality. What good reason is there to believe that it has *any* determinate, systematic answer? In the case of a naturalistic property, F-ness, that enters into laws of nature and causal relations, one can reasonably expect an answer to the question 'What things are F?'; for one can expect explanations of the laws in which F-ness participates. But in the case of rationality, especially from an emotivist perspective, no such reason exists for expecting a systematic theory. So it should not be surprising that no one has been able to think of a good one.

Besides the topics covered in this review, the book contains many substantial parts on which I have not commented. There is an evolutionary theory of the process by which our concept of rationality has evolved, a psychological theory of norm-acceptance and its relations to avowal, desire, and action, and a meta-ethical theory that explains moral notions in terms of when it is rational to feel guilt and shame. Gibbard's far-reaching discussions are subtle, ingenious, and well argued. The book is integrated and comprehensive, and provides a strong case for the emotivist perspective. It is not always easy going but well worth the effort: a must-read, in my view, for anyone concerned with normative issues.

9   Science and Art

I

Art and science are amongst our two most valuable and intriguing cultural practices; and in order to help understand them better it can be useful to scrutinize them in relation to one another. The present effort in that direction will be divided into two parts. First, I will mention some ways in which the arts and the sciences resemble and differ from each other. In particular, I will look sceptically at whether we can think of them as having the same goals—as both oriented towards truth, knowledge, and understanding. Second, I will compare them with respect to *autonomy*. I will note various respects in which science depends on extraneous factors and is therefore *not* autonomous. But I will then focus on a couple of respects in which it *is*: namely, the autonomy of its goal (to produce knowledge) and the autonomy of its means of achieving that goal (conformity with specifiable norms of rational inference and belief). Finally I will turn to the question of whether the arts are autonomous in these two respects; and my answer will be mixed. On the one hand, they have a singular aesthetic purpose which differs from those of other practices. But on the other hand, whether a certain work is held to fulfil that purpose tends to be highly subjective: it is regarded as doing so only when a characteristic aesthetic

For helpful discussion of the issues addressed here I would like to thank Samira Atallah, Ned Block, Paul Boghossian, Alison Denham, Pierre Jacob, Jerrold Katz, Mary Mothersill, Peter Pakesch, Martin Prinzhorn, Michael Ratledge, Marie-Noelle de Rohozinska, and Adele Schlombs.

satisfaction is provoked, which is contingent on a host of cultural and personal variables. Of course, this noncognitive goal and its correlated lack of autonomy are in no sense defects. On the contrary, the vibrancy and power of art depend on its distinctive function—one that leaves no room for norms of objective assessment.

II

Science is a socially vital practice with a history of thousands of years. It is conducted by specialists, who have undergone considerable training to become expert. It is divided into subpractices— e.g. physics, chemistry, biology, linguistics—and each scientist tends to concentrate on one or another of these areas. Norms (i.e. standards of quality) are applied to scientific work as to whether it is valuable, interesting, original, etc.; and a scientist recognized as especially talented can thereby achieve considerable wealth and fame.

At this high level of abstraction, art and science are barely distinguishable. Like science, art is a socially significant practice with an ancient history; it is conducted by highly trained specialists; it is divided into subpractices—painting, music, poetry, dance, and so on; it is assessed as valuable, original, and interesting; and it is capable of bringing substantial worldly rewards to those regarded as exceptionally proficient.

III

But now let us increase the magnification, looking more carefully at the goals, methods, and ultimate purposes of science and art; and let us see how far the parallels between them are preserved.

1. The goal of science is knowledge; knowledge of how the world works; knowledge of the laws of nature. Such knowledge is rightly valued for its own sake. But what sustains this sentiment is its utility: scientific knowledge enables us to predict and control our environment, and thereby to survive and flourish.

2. The various sciences are distinguished by reference to that part or aspect of the world they scrutinize: biology focuses on living things, physics on the fundamental elements of matter, psychology on the mind, etc. For each such domain there are basic principles governing the phenomena within it; and the job of the relevant science is to gain knowledge of those laws.

3. Knowledge has three main ingredients: belief, truth, and justification. That is to say: in order for one to qualify as *knowing* something, one must of course *believe* that it is the case, the belief must be *true*, and this true belief cannot be merely a lucky guess—one must be in possession of evidence that *justifies* it, that provides a good reason for having it. Therefore the immediate goal of a science is to be accomplished by its engendering beliefs of a certain special kind about the laws in its domain: namely, beliefs that are justified; beliefs that we have good reason to think are true.

4. The norm, or standard, or rule, that tells us whether a given belief is justified in science is roughly this:

   A belief is justified (rational, reasonable, legitimate) if it is part of a system of beliefs (an overall theory) that fits the observed facts and is relatively simple.

   Thus a new proposed theory is better than some current collection of beliefs—so that we ought to transfer our allegiance to it—when it exemplifies a higher degree of observational fit and simplicity.

5. This norm, specifying what a scientist *ought* to believe, is fairly constant across cultures and through time. Of course, what a given individual *actually* believes will be sometimes determined by various factors other than, and competing with, respect for this norm. A person may be subject to extreme political pressures or may be in the grip of self-interested ulterior motives, and such factors may engender beliefs that violate the norm of rationality. However, that norm is by and large respected.

6. As a consequence, science has arrived, through the centuries, at theories that are more and more observationally adequate and

simple. This is the sense in which science is *progressive*—the sense in which our current scientific beliefs are better than Newton's, and Newton's were better than Aristotle's.

IV

On all of these points the arts diverge radically from the sciences

(*a*) The various arts are not distinguished by reference to their focus on some distinctive part of the world but, rather, by reference to their concern with some distinctive sensory or cognitive faculty (or combination of such faculties) and their use of some distinctive medium. Thus, roughly speaking, painting is associated with vision and surfaces, sculpture with vision and three-dimensional objects, music with hearing, perfumery with smell, gastronomy with taste, fiction with the cognitive faculty of imagination and the medium of written language, etc.

(*b*) The goal of the arts is *not* the engendering of knowledge—of justified, true belief. The special point of a work of art is *not* to make a claim, to assert a proposition, to express some belief of the artist. Granted, an artwork—even a piece of music—may sometimes communicate something the artist believes, and may be intended to do so. But that does not provide its value as a work of art; it is not judged, qua *art*work, by reference to the truth or novelty of such a statement. The artist is not expected to provide *evidence* in support of his or her work. The terms of evaluation—whether the thing is beautiful or kitsch or gripping or boring or whatever—do not concern the plausibility of some theory that is being advanced. Michelangelo's *Brutus* attributes a certain appearance to him, but would not be less great if he did not in fact look that way. And the same goes for a piece of conceptual art. The correctness of what it might be intended to 'say' is not the point. Thus the arts, unlike the sciences, are not oriented towards belief, reason, truth, explanation, or understanding; and a work of art is not primarily assessed in terms of its possession of these characteristics.

(c) Instead, the goal of the arts would seem to be something special, which we call 'aesthetic value'. Of course, this is to offer merely a label, and it would be desirable to have an account of what that label stands for—or at least an account of how we go about judging whether something has that mysterious quality. I have little to say on this hard and important topic. But one thing we can be confident of—or so I have just argued—is the negative point that aesthetic value is *not* the same thing as knowledge or rational justification or truth. Whatever may be the basis for our assessment of works of art, it is certainly not the same as the norm we deploy in the evaluation of scientific beliefs.

(d) Generalizing this point, a particular artist (or school) may be oriented towards some particular moral, political, spiritual, practical, or epistemological goal. But the resulting works are not assessed as *art* by reference to the desirability of such a goal or by reference to their effectiveness in promoting it. The primary focus of evaluation of the work is in terms of its *aesthetic* merits. One can disagree with the goal and/or be sceptical of the work's chances of accomplishing it, yet still be impressed with its quality as a work of art.

(e) Not only does aesthetic judgement pay no attention to epistemological standards; but whereas the product of a scientist—namely, some recommendation about what to believe—is always combined with an explicit account of why such belief is appropriate (i.e. of how it meets the above-mentioned norm of reason), the artist on the other hand tends simply to present his or her work with the presumption that it has aesthetic value (whatever that may be exactly), but without any attempt to show why it does. The artist is not expected to explain or defend himself or herself.

(*f*) There may of course be discussion by *critics* of whether some work of art is or is not good—of why it does, or does not, or should, or should not, produce the proper aesthetic response. But it is striking how much disagreement there is about what the standards of evaluation (if any) should be, and also how much disagreement there can be about whether a thing is aesthetically valuable. And, unlike in science, such disagreements very often remain unresolved.

(*g*) These two characteristics of art—there being no requirement of justification, and the extent of disagreement—suggest that the arts do not rely on objective norms of assessment. It would seem rather that aesthetic judgement results from something like the following process. In the first place, the artwork gives rise to a complex experience involving immediate sensations, associated memories and thoughts, and feelings and emotions (such as delight, excitement, disgust, or being moved to tears). In the second place, this experience engenders (and then incorporates) a distinctively aesthetic feeling of satisfaction or dissatisfaction, where (and this is the crucial point) that reaction is not guided by, or subject to, standards or norms. And finally, a positive or negative aesthetic judgement is made in order to give expression to that feeling: the work is held to be valuable or not. Thus, the experience of an artwork either works on a person or not, either it gives the aesthetic buzz or it doesn't, and diverse judgements of quality or value are made accordingly; but no objective relevant considerations can be cited to *justify* such judgements. Doubtless, a critic or educator may help someone to derive from the artwork the appropriate experience, may help them to see or hear it as intended. But the vital further effect—aesthetic pleasure—either occurs or not, independently of explanations or guidance from experts.

(*h*) The claim that art lacks objective norms is admittedly something of an oversimplification, but not much of one. There would seem to be a few fairly objective general norms of assessment relating, for example, to (i) technical expertise, (ii) originality, and (iii) the range of people over which the artwork is effective. But these are surely peripheral and secondary. The *central* ground of someone's positive aesthetic judgement is his experience of aesthetic satisfaction, and that appears to be a highly subjective and contingent matter.

(*i*) One might attempt some specification of the characteristics that, for a given person and culture and type of art, are conducive to the *production* of aesthetic pleasure. And the results of such an investigation might be articulated as directions for how to construct something that works. But such principles are not norms of assessment. Moreover they are bound to be extremely local and incomplete. Separate art-forms and periods will call for separate advice manuals, and they could never be more than crude guidelines—there will surely never be a foolproof recipe.

(*j*) In so far as there is no objective standard of 'better' or 'worse' in art, there can be no objective progress. Someone might happen to prefer contemporary installations to impressionism, and impressionism to Renaissance painting—and might then have the feeling of progress. But someone else will have the opposite preferences, and there is no sense in supposing that either of these views is objectively correct. This is not to deny that judgements of aesthetic value may appropriately be labelled 'true' or 'false': as in any domain, the claim that a judgement is true asserts barely more than the judgement itself. What is denied is that scientific and aesthetic theses have the same prospect of justification, hence the same prospect of progress.

V

Now let me turn to the second part of my discussion, leading to the question of whether art is autonomous. In order to help clarify this question, consider the corresponding issue as it arises in connection with the sciences. What would it *mean* for us to ask whether chemistry, for example, is autonomous? Obviously we would be asking whether certain aspects of this subject are independent of certain other matters? But which aspects and which matters?

Clearly the activity of doing modern chemistry requires a certain social structure, certain economic conditions, and so on. In that sense chemistry is *not* autonomous: the practice could not exist in isolation.

Also, the selection of which topics within chemistry are practically important, and decisions about which experiments are safe, and morally acceptable and not too expensive, depend on political and ethical priorities. So there is a further respect in which this subject is *not* autonomous.

Third, the theoretical conjectures that occur to a scientist may well be stimulated by external factors—by a symphony, a dream, what happens to be seen while walking down the street, etc. Again, we find a certain *lack* of autonomy.

But fourth, and focusing now on the immediate *goal* of chemistry (which is to discover the laws within its domain), that goal is distinctive and independent of other practices. Thus we have finally identified a respect in which chemistry is autonomous. And this is related to another one: the norms for assessing theoretical proposals. Whether or not a certain theory in chemistry should be believed will admittedly depend on the situation in physics. However, if one considers science as a *whole*, the above-emphasized norm of theoretical justification—the preference for observational fit and simplicity—dictates that whether a scientific belief is reasonable does not depend on anything outside science itself.

Moreover, since scientific theorizing is predominantly rational—i.e. since it does more or less conform to this norm of reason—then one can say that the evolution of science is fairly autonomous. In other words, two cultures with different ethical proclivities, different political systems, and different aesthetic sensibilities, would (given the same body of observed facts) be expected to arrive at more or less the same scientific theories. Thus one should resist those critics of 'Western science' who emphasize its embedding within a specific socio-cultural context and proceed to draw relativistic conclusions about the impossibility of objective knowledge and progress. For the above-mentioned norm of reason is universally acknowledged, at least implicitly: i.e. those theories that *work* (providing the ability to predict and control) are generally believed.

VI

How about the arts? Clearly they also depend on other practices in all the various ways that we have seen that the sciences do. The existence of orchestral music requires certain social and economic conditions. An installation may be too dangerous or morally abhorrent or expensive to be implemented. An artist, like a scientist, may get ideas from anywhere at all.

But the interesting question is whether there are nevertheless residual respects—concerning goals, and standards for determining when they are met—in which the arts *are* autonomous? In the case of the sciences the answer was yes: their aim, knowledge, is autonomous; whether we have achieved it in a given case is objectively decidable, for the norms that will engender it are universally respected. As a result, the historical development of the sciences is fairly independent of other causal factors. But in the arts the situation is somewhat different.

Vis-à-vis goals, the arts are just as autonomous as the sciences. The production of aesthetic value is distinctive and independent of the goals of other cultural practices. Surely nothing besides music can do for us what music does. And the same thing goes for literature, film, dance, and the rest.

However, *vis-à-vis* judgements regarding whether these goals have been achieved, there would appear to be a relative lack of objectivity and autonomy in the arts. Granted, the aesthetic response to certain exceptional artworks is impressively invariable, perhaps determined by human nature. But such cases are rare. Much of the music and literature and painting that is prized in one culture is not especially appreciated in another, even after appropriate exposure to it. And there are also enormous variations of taste within cultures. This contingency and variability in the production of aesthetic pleasure would seem to be tied to the above-noted fact that assessment in the arts is only minimally governed by norms. Beyond considerations of technique, inventiveness, and popularity, there remains the most important thing—the production of aesthetic pleasure—for which the very idea of a guiding norm is absurd. Instead, whether an artwork gives aesthetic pleasure to a person would appear to depend on a myriad of external facts about that person—facts that vary within and across cultures.

VII

In summary, what I have been suggesting is that science and art differ significantly from one another with respect to the issue of autonomy. In the case of science, despite its interaction with other practices, there is a constant and essential and sufficient principle of evaluation, as a result of which science evolves, to a first approximation, independently of external influences. However, the practice of art incorporates no such norm; aesthetic value is attributed on the basis of aesthetic pleasure; but what will produce that desired effect varies enormously across individuals, times, and cultures as a highly complex and unknown function of external factors. This is why, although Einstein's theories improve on Newton's, and Chomsky's improve on Bloomfield's, one shrinks from speaking of such progress in the transition from Rembrandt to Matisse, Mozart to Prokofiev, or Shakespeare to Brecht. Not of course that one doesn't have preferences, and not that one can say nothing about why one has them. But there is no established context-independent norm by which the correctness of such choices may be settled.

10 Wittgenstein's Meta-philosophical Development

It is often said that Wittgenstein gave us two utterly distinct and contradictory philosophies, issuing from two radically different views of meaning: supposedly, the first of these philosophies, contained in his *Tractatus Logico-Philosophicus* (1922), comes out of the theory that the meaning of a word is its *referent*; and the second one, articulated in the *Philosophical Investigations* (1953), comes out of a *use*-theory of meaning. The main purpose of the present paper is to oppose this picture and to advocate an alternative. I will argue that the basis of Wittgenstein's thought was always his view of what *philosophy* is rather than his view of what *meaning* is. From that perspective we can see the key defect in the *Tractatus* as a certain relatively small incoherence within its *meta*-philosophy, and we will be able to explain the central ideas of the *Investigations* as what emerge when this mistake is rectified. If that is right, then we ought to think of the *Tractatus* as providing a sort of flawed first draft of his mature position, rather than a profoundly different and wholly rejected point of view.

Let us begin with a different, more widely discussed issue— another apparent incoherence in the *Tractatus*. Consider the well-known passage from the end of the book, where Wittgenstein acknowledges that much of what has come before is by its own lights 'senseless', but tries to remove the sting from this concession

For helpful discussion I would like to thank David Pears, Meredith Williams, Michael Williams, Thomas Ricketts, and James Conant.

by suggesting that these problematic earlier remarks can nonetheless help us to see things properly:

6.54 My propositions are elucidatory in this way: he who understands me finally recognizes them as senseless, when he has climbed out through them, on them, over them. (He must so to speak throw away the ladder, after he has climbed up on it).
He must surmount these propositions; then he sees the world rightly.

Naturally, the question arises as to whether the metaphor that Wittgenstein offers us here succeeds in rescuing his position. For how can anyone consistently endorse certain propositions and at the same time categorize them as senseless? Is not his resort to the image of 'using a ladder and then throwing it away' merely a vain attempt to mask a fatal difficulty?

In order to address this problem we need to be a little more concrete about it. In the course of the *Tractatus* Wittgenstein makes a series of interconnected pronouncements on grammar, meaning, metaphysics, and metaphilosophy. He claims, or seems to claim:

• Regarding *grammar*: that each 'proposition' (i.e. sentence + meaning) is constructed in the course of the following procedure: (i) combine primitive terms ('names') with one another to form elementary propositions; (ii) operate on these with 'not', 'and', 'every', etc., to form logically complex propositions; and (iii) introduce defined terms for the sake of abbreviation. Consequently, each proposition will have a definite basic content that may be articulated in terms of primitives and logical constants.
• Regarding *meaning*: that each name refers to a simple 'object'; that each elementary proposition 'depicts' a possible 'atomic' fact (and is true if and only if that fact exists); and that the meaning ('sense') of every other proposition is a function which yields a truth value for each possible combination of truth values assigned to the elementary propositions.
• Regarding *metaphysics*: that each possible atomic fact is a possible configuration of simple objects; and that the world—the collection

of all actual facts—is determined by which such possibilities are realized and which are not.

- And regarding *meta-philosophy*: that philosophical questions and answers are disguised nonsense; they look meaningful but turn out to have no basic content (for they are not constructible by means of the three-stage procedure mentioned above). Therefore one should not engage in philosophical theorizing, but merely debunk, through conceptual analysis, other people's attempts to do so.

I will call this collection of pronouncements 'The *Tractatus* Theory' or 'T³'. Now, returning to the 'ladder' problem, is there not a contradiction between Wittgenstein's claim that T³ is senseless and his claim that it can nonetheless help us to see the world rightly? How can T³ possibly articulate a correct view of things or rationally persuade us of anything—even of its own meaninglessness—if it doesn't make sense?

Wittgenstein has available to him a partially effective response to these sceptical questions. What he can say is (*a*) that the sort of 'senselessness' displayed by T³ is not so extreme as to preclude its having logical consequences; therefore (*b*) that 'senselessness', in the present context, is not to be equated with utter gibberish, but rather with logical incoherence; (*c*) that supposing T³ to be correct is indeed 'senseless' (in this weak respect), for it leads to contradiction—it is the basis for a *reductio ad absurdum*; and (*d*) that the moral of this *reductio* argument is that the semantic and metaphysical concepts (such as *reference* and *object*) deployed T³ in are self-contradictory.[1] But although this reading will explain how T³ might have a certain import, we are still left in the dark as to how these propositions—if

---

[1] Wittgenstein probably had in mind the paradoxes (concerning e.g. the concept HORSE) that seem inevitably to arise within the Fregean view of *reference*, a view which he may have regarded as definitive of the notion. For example, since 'the concept HORSE' is a singular term, it can only refer to an *object*, therefore certainly not to a *concept*; so we can infer that the concept HORSE is not a concept! See Gottlob Frege, 'Concept and Object', *Translations from the Philosophical Writings of Gottlob Frege*, ed. P. Geach and M. Black (Oxford, Blackwell, 1952); and also Peter Geach, 'Saying and Showing in Frege and Wittgenstein', *Acta Philosophica Fennica*, 28 1–3 (1976).

they are indeed internally inconsistent—could enable us to 'see the world rightly'. With respect to that issue there are two principal directions of interpretation. Perhaps Wittgenstein felt that, even though T³'s ontological doctrines cannot be coherently stated in the way it tries to, there is nonetheless something right about them—something that cannot properly be *said* but is *shown* (i.e. is implicit in grammatical structure). But in that case he would be taking himself to have somehow managed to articulate what cannot really be articulated! Alternatively, his view was that there is *no* way of saving T³'s semantic and metaphysical doctrines and that they (including the show/say distinction) have to be completely rejected—though not as absolute nonsense. But in that case why does Wittgenstein announce (in his Preface) that the fundamental aim of his book is to 'set limits to thought' (as is done by T³)? And why does he refer (in the *Philosophical Investigations*) to the "grave mistake" of his earlier work, and proceed to give a systematic critique of its central tenets? It seems to me that the less objectionable of these two readings is the first one. Thus we are left attributing to Wittgenstein a highly implausible doctrine: namely, that what cannot be said might nonetheless be shown. So there is indeed something incoherent in his quasi-endorsement of propositions that cannot be straightforwardly asserted.[2]

[2] Commentary on the *Tractatus* tends to be divided these days between advocates of the so-called Standard Interpretation, according to which Wittgenstein *endorses* T³ while recognizing that some of its elements cannot be *said* but merely *shown*, and proponents of the more recent so-called Resolute Interpretation, according to which he rejects T³'s metaphysical and semantic pronouncements as plain nonsense. My own sympathies, as indicated in the text, are with the standard view. I think that Wittgenstein should not be read as maintaining that the propositions of T³ are nothing but mumbo-jumbo. And I think that he—probably wrongly—takes that theory to be somehow pointing towards the truth. Note that on this point I have changed my position from the one expressed in the first published version of this paper—where I suggested that Wittgenstein *thoroughly* rejected T³.

For the Standard Interpretation see Frank Ramsey 'Critical Notice of L. Wittgenstein's Tractatus Logico-Philosophicus', *Mind*, NS 32/128 (Oct. 1923), 465–78; Max Black, *A Companion to Wittgenstein's Tractatus* (Cambridge: Cambridge University Press, 1964); Elisabeth Anscombe, *An Introduction to Wittgenstein's Tractatus* (London: Hutchinson, 1959); Peter Hacker, 'Was He Trying to Whistle it?', in Alice Crary and Rupert Read (eds.), *The New Wittgenstein* (London: Routledge, 2000);

However, there is a further and deeper threat of incoherence within Wittgenstein's position—one that would not be relieved by a show/say distinction, even if such a thing could be made out. Namely, there is a conflict between, on the one hand, his anti-theoretical meta-philosophical dictum to the effect that philosophy can do no more than expose pseudo-questions for what they are, and, on the other hand, the idea—embodied in the grammatical and logical doctrines that are developed for the diagnosis and treatment of such pseudo-questions—that one can legitimately produce philosophical theories of considerable intellectual value. Thus Wittgenstein prohibits philosophical theorizing on the basis of a philosophical theory. This tension is quite distinct from the one that he acknowledges and addresses in his 'ladder' paragraph. And it is an incontrovertible incoherence—no subtle distinction, clever metaphor, or other form of fancy footwork, is going to be able to get him out of it.

What he has to do to resolve this difficulty, and what he *does* eventually do in the *Philosophical Investigations,* is to make a small but significant change in his view of what philosophy is—retaining most of it, but abandoning the component that is responsible for the internal conflict. Let us see how this is accomplished.

The *Tractatus* meta-philosophy involves the following sequence of ideas:

(1) Philosophical questions are provoked by confusion (rather than by ignorance, which is the source of *scientific* questions).

David Pears, *The False Prison,* i (Oxford: Oxford University Press, 1987); Geach, 'Saying and Showing'; and Norman Malcolm, *Ludwig Wittgenstein: A Memoir* (2nd edn. Oxford: Oxford University Press, 1974). For the Resolute Interpretation see Cora Diamond, 'Throwing Away the Ladder: How to Read the *Tractatus*', in her *The Realistic Spirit* (Cambridge Mass.: MIT Press, 1991); Thomas Ricketts, 'Pictures, Logic, and the Limits of Sense in Wittgenstein's *Tractatus*', in H. Sluga and D. Dunn (eds.), *The Cambridge Companion to Wittgenstein* (Cambridge: Cambridge University Press, 1996), 57–73; Warren Goldfarb, 'Metaphysics and Nonsense: On Cora Diamond's *The Realistic Spirit*', *Journal of Philosophical Research,* 22 (1997), 57–74; and James Conant 'Must We Show What We Cannot Say', in R. Fleming and M. Paine (eds.), *The Senses of Stanley Cavell* (Lewisburg, Pa.: Bucknell University Press, 1989), 242–83.

(2) Therefore, they articulate pseudoproblems, which can at best be eliminated not solved.

(3) Consequently, no philosophical explanations, theories, or discoveries are possible.

(4) Philosophical confusions originate in misunderstandings about language.

(5) To be more specific, such confusions arise because of the considerable distances between the superficial forms of certain propositions and their ultimate analyses in terms of fundamental primitives. For example, 'The F is G' should be analysed, following Russell, as '($\exists$x)(Fx & (y)(Fy $\rightarrow$ x = y) & Gx)'. This distance can be so great that we can easily fail to appreciate a statement's real meaning. And in the case of certain statements, we fail to appreciate their complete lack of meaning.

It seems clear that the incoherence with which we are now concerned stems from the conflict between the *anti*-theoretical import of (1), (2), (3), and (4), and the detailed *theoretical* diagnosis of philosophical confusion that is offered in (5). For that diagnosis is based on a substantive philosophical theory of language: namely, that each proposition has an ultimate conceptual analysis to be provided in certain specified terms.

Consequently, Wittgenstein can hang on to the heart and the bulk of his meta-philosophy, but avoid the tension within it, if he gives up his theory-laden account in (5) of the way in which we are confused by language, and replaces it with an alternative. And this is exactly what he comes to do.[3] The meta-philosophy of the *Investigations* keeps (1), (2), (3), and (4). Thus Wittgenstein continues to hold that philosophical puzzlement derives from illusions

[3] Even though Wittgenstein does not himself draw attention to it, the incoherence in the *Tractatus* on which I am focusing is so serious and glaring that he surely must have become aware of it and must have been motivated (in part) by it to modify his meta-philosophical position.

engendered by language; and so he continues to hold that philosophy cannot yield knowledge. But he comes to see that the precise source of our linguogenic misunderstanding is not the gap between superficial grammatical form and 'underlying logical form'—a notion which he abandons—but is rather something with no theoretical presuppositions: namely, our tendency to be mesmerized by linguistic analogies. More specifically, he replaces (5) with

(5*) Philosophical confusion resides in the tendency to over-stretch analogies in the uses of words, to be unnecessarily perplexed by the conceptual tensions that result, and to wrongly feel that an a priori theory of the phenomenon in question is needed to demystify it.

To elaborate this a little: his idea is that the words in a certain small class (e.g. the numerals) are seen to function in many respects like the words in another more prominent class (e.g. names of physical objects); however we tend to overlook the differences and, as a consequence, are inclined to raise improper (hence unanswerable) questions about the phenomena characterized by terms in the smaller class. We thereby fall into conceptual bewilderment, into an impression that these phenomena are extraordinarily weird; and the cure appears to be an appropriate a priori account of them. But, according to Wittgenstein, the peculiar puzzlement we feel is one from which no *theory* can adequately deliver us. What is needed, rather, is a rooting out of its irrational sources. Moreover, besides being unmotivated, any a priori theory that we might be tempted to propose is bound to be defective in one way or another, depending on what sort of theory it is. For if we insist on the legitimacy of the questions, then the impossibility of answering them will lead to either scepticism or revisionism about the phenomena—and both sorts of theory are vitiated by the over-stretched analogies on which they rely. On the other hand, if the questions are abandoned, then our continued demand for a substantive a priori theory (designed to rationalize their illegitimacy) will yield either a systematization of intuitions that has no explanatory value or, even worse, a senseless metaphysical inflation of truisms.

For example, the numerals function in many ways like names of physical objects. Therefore, overlooking the important differences, we are tempted to ask the sort of questions about the things that numerals designate (i.e. numbers) that we ask about the referents of other names: Where are the numbers? What are they made of? How can we interact with them? And if we can't, how is it possible to know anything about them? The traditional way of responding to such puzzles is to develop versions of the four sorts of a priori theory just mentioned—theories such as (a) the skeptical, 'Numbers don't exist, although it's useful to pretend they do' (Fictionalism); (b) the revisionist, 'Mathematical reality can't be the way it is naively conceived to be, as existing independently of human thought' (Constructivism); (c) the systematic, 'Mathematical facts may be derived from logical facts' (Logicism); or (d) the metaphysical, 'Numbers are not in space and time, but are nonetheless REAL objects' (Platonism). But from Wittgenstein's point of view these 'theoretical' responses are unwarranted (each in their own way) and take the questions more seriously than they deserve to be taken, given their confused origin. The right reaction to our puzzlement is to expose and eliminate the mistakes that provoke it—that is, to recognize how the questions derive from the exaggeration of linguistic analogies, how the puzzlement they induce is un-called-for, and how the theories designed to dispel that puzzlement are irrational. Once this has been done we will be left with no new knowledge—with no positive 'philosophy of mathematics'—but merely with a strengthened resistance to philosophical confusion.

Thus, as in the *Tractatus*, there can be no philosophical theories, explanations, or discoveries. But whereas in that book the diagnosis of philosophical confusion adverted to a sophisticated philosophical theory of language—rendering the overall account incoherent as we have seen—the later meta-philosophy does not presuppose any such theory. It is fully anti-theoretical. The inconsistency has been removed.

But is this really so? Has the original difficulty really been avoided? It would seem that the *Investigations* faces a conflict of exactly the same kind as we found in the *Tractatus*: namely, a contradiction between an anti-theoretical meta-philosophy and the view—which is surely a highly debatable *theory*—that philosophical problems are provoked by a specified form of linguistic confusion?

However, in the present context, unlike before, I do think that a bit of fancy footwork can help. What we might say on behalf of Wittgenstein is that his view of the nature of philosophical problems is indeed debatable, but nonetheless concerns matters that are not *theoretical*, i.e. not *hidden* from us. The distinction required here is that between, on the one hand, the *obvious, undeniable,* and *uncontroversial* and, on the other hand, what is *open to view*—where phenomena of the latter sort may remain unnoticed by those who are, for whatever reasons, not looking in the right direction. If philosophical problems really do derive, as Wittgenstein asserts, from a familiar species of linguistic confusion, then this is a phenomenon of the second kind. We should be able to *see*, both in particular cases and in general, how linguistic analogies can easily produce conceptual tensions; how these tensions, when their source is unrecognized, will result in confusion; and how the alternate theoretical responses to such confusion will be unmotivated and irrational. These points may not in fact be obvious to everyone; but, according to Wittgenstein, they can be made so with the help of well-chosen hints, illustrations, and alterations of perspective.[4] Thus Wittgenstein's later meta-philosophy is not, in his sense, a 'theory'; so there is no contradiction in its condemnation of such things.

---

[4] See *Investigations*, § 92, where Wittgenstein contrasts the sort of non-theoretical account that he wishes *now* to give with the theory that was offered in the *Tractatus*: 'if we too in these investigations are trying to understand the essence of language—its function, its structure—yet *this* is not what those [*Tractatus*] questions have in view. For they see in the essence, not something that lies open to view and that becomes surveyable by rearrangement, but something that lies *beneath* the surface. Something that lies within, which we see when we look *into* the thing, and which an analysis digs out.'

The improvement in Wittgenstein's meta-philosophy to which I am drawing attention—the change from (5) to (5*)—lies at the bottom of the other major differences between the *Tractatus* and the *Investigations*. Most importantly, it explains the huge emphasis that he comes to place on the fact that the various words in a language are used in extremely different ways. From the very outset of the *Investigations*, and throughout that work, we are advised to give characterizations of language that describe how idiosyncratically the different words are used—and not to be concerned with their referents or psychological concomitants. His point is not that theories of these other kinds would be incoherent or false or that they could serve no purpose at all, but that they are not what are needed for the effective disposal of philosophical problems. For in so far as these problems result from insufficient attention to linguistic variation—from the exaggeration of linguistic analogies—they must be treated by providing pertinent reminders of the divergent ways that terms are actually deployed.

It is crucial to appreciate the difference between this aspect of the *Investigations*—the focus on word-use—and a related but quite distinct point: namely, Wittgenstein's identification of the meaning of a word with its use. It is one thing to say, for the reason mentioned above, that philosophical illumination will be promoted by attending to how words are used, and quite a different thing to say that the meaning of a word consists in its use in the language. The first of these points evidently plays the predominant role in determining Wittgenstein's approach to particular philosophical problems—the problems that surround our notions of experience, mathematics, knowledge, art, and so on; and also that surround our notion of meaning. But it is the second point that is usually emphasized by commentators on Wittgenstein. Indeed, it has been given much more weight in his later thinking than it deserves.

For notice, to start with, that it is far from obvious that Wittgenstein changed his mind much about the nature of meaning *en route* from the *Tractatus* to the *Investigations*. After all, he explicitly acknowledges that the word 'meaning' is ambiguous: *Investigations*, § 43 defines meaning as use, but only 'For a large class of cases—though not all—in which we employ the word "meaning" '. Clearly he is not—as is often wrongly supposed— saying that it is only the meanings of *some* words that may be iden- tified with their uses. Rather, he is allowing that there are various cases in which, in speaking of a word's 'meaning', we have in mind something else—for example, its referent, or its pragmatic force, or some concurrent intention. And this observation squares perfectly well with the *Tractatus* emphasis on meaning qua referent. Thus Wittgenstein's use conception of meaning does not contradict his *Tractatus* position. His change of view concerns, not what meaning is, but which brand of meaning is philosophically important.[5]

Nor can credit be given to Wittgenstein's definition as the source of his new meta-philosophy. For in fact that meta-philosophy can- not (and need not) be derived from the use conception of meaning. It is often claimed, on the contrary, that Wittgenstein's objection to traditional philosophy as 'language on holiday' stems precisely from the idea that meaning consists in (and is therefore confined by) ordinary usage.[6] The reasoning attributed to him goes roughly as follows:

(i) Meaning = use.
(ii) Therefore any deployment of a word beyond its ordinary usage would be meaningless.
(iii) But philosophical theorizing does involve departures from ordinary usage.
(iv) Therefore philosophical theories are meaningless.

---

[5] The main target of the opening remarks of the *Investigations* is not the *Tractatus* view that each primitive term has a referent; but is rather the allegedly Augustinian position which adds to this that these referential meanings are learnt by *ostensive definition*.

[6] See e.g. David Pears, *The False Prison*, ii (Oxford: Oxford University Press, 1987); and Jerrold Katz, *The Metaphysics of Meaning*, (Cambridge, Mass.: MIT Press, 1991).

(v) Therefore we must confine ourselves to removing the temptation to engage in philosophical theorizing.

But this line of thought is glaringly invalid—specifically the step from (i) to (ii). If that move were allowed then the consequences would be far more radical than could have been intended by Wittgenstein, or than can be accepted by us. In particular, the recognition of past errors in *any* domain would be impossible, and even *scientific* theorizing would be incoherent. Let me elaborate these two implications.

In the first place, a vital constraint on how the term 'use' must be understood in the context of Wittgenstein's account of meaning is that there be the possibility of appreciating that we have until now been saying (and thinking) false things,—i.e. applying words incorrectly. It must be possible to discover that certain common uses of words are in fact mistaken. (For example, we have now learnt that we were wrong to say, 'The sun revolves around the Earth'.) But in that case, the notion of 'use' that Wittgenstein needs cannot imply that a philosophical theory, solely in virtue of its departures from what is ordinarily said, would have to be meaningless. In other words, the use conception of meaning leaves it open that philosophy is amongst those disciplines that enable us to discover errors in accepted usage.

And in the second place, although an everyday word might be deployed in a novel way within the context of a philosophical theory, it will nonetheless have *some* use within that theory. Therefore the use conception—far from condemning the word as having become meaningless—will certify that it still *does* have a meaning (albeit a novel one). This sort of commandeering of terms is common in science: familiar words (such as 'energy', 'fish', and 'language') are pressed into unfamiliar, explanatory service and thereby given new and technical meanings. So why shouldn't it happen within philosophy too? And in that case, why should metaphysical theories be any less intelligible that scientific ones?

Thus the identification of meaning with use cannot get us to the conclusion that philosophical theorizing is misconceived. However, no such inference is needed. The real basis for Wittgenstein's meta-philosophy is the observation of so many problems whose sources turn out to be linguistic overgeneralization. He need not, and should not, go so far as to say that the theories proposed as solutions to these pseudo-problems are invariably meaningless. It suffices to recognize that, even when meaningful, such theoretical claims are not properly motivated and are not justified.

From this metaphilosophical perspective the problems surrounding the phenomenon, X, must be treated by focusing on the special ways that the term 'X' is used. And applying that methodology to the phenomenon of meaning, we will see that words are said to have 'the same meaning' when their basic use is the same, and that a grasp of the meaning of a word is attributed to someone when he is able to use it appropriately. That is, we arrive at the identification of the meaning of a word with its use. Thus the direction of thought is from Wittgenstein's meta-philosophy to his use conception of meaning rather than the other way around.[7]

To summarize: I have been arguing that, early and late, it is Wittgenstein's view of philosophy, rather than his view of meaning, that plays the pivotal role in his thought. His account of meaning has few significant implications and does not undergo substantial revision. His meta-philosophy is what is central and revolutionary. It does change somewhat—an incoherent element is removed from it and replaced—and this modification gives rise to considerable differences in the way that specific philosophical problems are treated. But the correction in his core meta-philosophical position is small in relation to all that is retained: namely, that philosophical questioning is provoked by linguogenic confusion, that it should not be straightforwardly answered, and that it cannot yield philosophical knowledge. Thus the *Tractatus* and the *Investigations* represent improving expressions of one and the same hyper-deflationary insight.

[7] Note that the philosophical problems about meaning that Wittgenstein addresses in the *Investigations* are not intended to be solved by reference to the use conception. On the contrary, these problems arise from the difficulty of seeing how meaning, *given* its determination of, and by, an extensive body of usage, can be 'grasped in a flash'. They are to be solved by attending to our use of the words 'grasp', 'determine', etc.

Initial Publication of the Essays

The present essays are slightly revised versions of the following papers:

Essay 1 was first published as 'Three Forms of Realism', *Synthese*, 5 (1982), 181–201.

Essay 2 was first published as 'Realism and Truth', *Philosophical Perspectives*, 10: 'Metaphysics', ed. J. Tomberlin (1996), 187–97.

Essay 3 was first published as 'How to Choose between Empirically Indistinguishable Theories', *Journal of Philosophy*, 79/2 (1982), 61–77.

Essay 4 was first published as 'Meaning, Use, and Truth', *Mind*, 104. 414 (Apr. 1995), 355–68.

Essay 5 was first published as 'On the Nature and Norms of Theoretical Commitment', *Philosophy of Science*, 58/1 (1991), 1–14.

Essay 6 was first published as 'Wittgensteinian Bayesianism', *Midwest Studies in Philosophy*, 18, ed. P. French, T. Uehling, and H. Wettstein (Notre Dame, Ind.: University of Notre Dame Press, 1993), 62–77.

Essay 7 was first published as a review of J. R. Lucas's *The Future* (Oxford: Blackwell, 1989), *British Journal for the Philosophy of Science*, 44 (1993), 579–83.

Essay 8 was first published as 'Gibbard's Theory of Norms', *Philosophy and Public Affairs*, 22/1, (1993), 67–78.

Essay 9 was first published as 'Science and Art', in Peter Pakesch (ed.), *Die Autonomie in der Kunst*, (Basel, Kunsthalle, 2001), 67–76.

Essay 10 was first published as 'Wittgenstein's Meta-Philosophical Development', in M. Kolbel and B. Weiss (eds.), *Wittgenstein's Lasting Significance* (London: Routledge, 2004); presented at the Gregynog Wittgenstein Conference in July 2001 and at the Kirchberg Wittgenstein Conference in August 2001.

I would like to thank the various original publishers of these papers for allowing me to reprint them.

Index